GREAT EXPECTATIONS

The *Oxford Progressive English Readers* series provides a wide range of reading for learners of English.

Each book in the series has been written to follow the strict guidelines of a syllabus, wordlist and structure list. The texts are graded according to these guidelines; Grade 1 at a 1,400 word level, Grade 2 at a 2,100 word level, Grade 3 at a 3,100 word level, Grade 4 at a 3,700 word level and Grade 5 at a 5,000 word level.

The latest methods of text analysis, using specially designed software, ensure that readability is carefully controlled at every level. Any new words which are vital to the mood and style of the story are explained within the text, and reoccur throughout for maximum reinforcement. New language items are also clarified by attractive illustrations.

Each book has a short section containing carefully graded exercises and controlled activities, which test both global and specific understanding.

Great Expectations

Charles Dickens

Hong Kong
Oxford University Press
Oxford

Oxford University Press

Oxford   New York
Athens   Auckland   Bangkok   Bombay
Calcutta   Cape Town   Dar es Salaam   Delhi
Florence   Hong Kong   Istanbul   Karachi
Kuala Lumpur   Madras   Madrid   Melbourne
Mexico City   Nairobi   Paris   Singapore
Taipei   Tokyo   Toronto

and associated companies in
Berlin   Ibadan

Oxford is a trade mark of Oxford University Press

First published 1993
This impression (lowest digit)
7   9   10   8   6

Illustrated by K. Y. Chan

Syllabus designer: David Foulds

Text processing and analysis by Luxfield Consultants Ltd

ISBN 0 19 585453 5

Printed in Hong Kong
Published by Oxford University Press (China) Ltd
18/F Warwick House East, Taikoo Place, 979 King's Road,
Quarry Bay, Hong Kong

CONTENTS

1 THE ESCAPED PRISONER   1

2 CHRISTMAS DAY   9

3 MISS HAVISHAM   17

4 JOE'S APPRENTICE   26

5 BIDDY   34

6 IN LONDON WITH HERBERT   41

7 A VERY UNEXPECTED VISITOR   48

8 PROVIS TELLS HIS STORY   57

9 PROVIS GOES INTO HIDING   65

10 ON THE RIVER   72

11 THE BEST OF FRIENDS   79

    QUESTIONS AND ACTIVITIES   85

THE ESCAPED PRISONER

In the churchyard

It was a cold, wet and grey afternoon, almost evening.
I was alone in the churchyard near my home. My father,
mother and five brothers had all died, and were buried
in that place. I had gone to the churchyard to look at 5
their graves.

Beyond were the marshes: dark, flat fields with
streams running between them. I could see a few cows
here and there, eating the grass, but I could see no
people anywhere. Further beyond the fields was the 10
river. A cold wind was blowing in from the sea.

As I sat in that sad, dark, lonely place, I began to
feel afraid. I started to cry.

'Stop that noise!' a fierce voice suddenly shouted.

A man jumped out from among the
gravestones. He was wearing
rough, dirty clothes. His shoes
were old and worn out. He
had no hat or coat. On
his leg was a heavy
iron chain. He was
an escaped prisoner.
Before I could run
away, he caught
hold of me.

'Keep still, you
little devil, or I'll
cut your throat!'
he shouted.

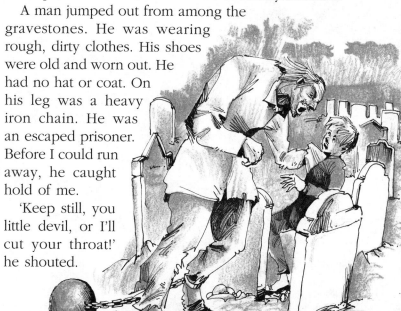

'Please, don't cut my throat, sir!' I cried, terrified. 'Don't kill me!'

'Tell me your name then!' said the man. 'Quick now!'

'Pip, sir.'

'Pip, is it?' He searched through my pockets, which contained only a piece of bread. He ate the bread hungrily, as if he had not eaten for many days. I fell onto the ground, trembling with fear.

'You young dog,' growled the prisoner, 'what fat cheeks you have! Maybe I'll eat you, too! Now look here. Where's your mother?'

'There, sir,' I said.

He jumped up and started to run away.

The cruel young man

When the prisoner saw that no one was following him, he stopped and looked back.

'My mother is there, sir,' I said, pointing to her grave. 'And my father is beside her.'

'Ah!' he said, coming back. 'Then who do you live with?'

'My sister, sir, Mrs Joe Gargery. She's married to Joe Gargery, the blacksmith. I live with them at the forge, sir.'

'Blacksmith, eh?' He looked down at the chain on his leg, and then he looked at me. 'A blacksmith will have tools for cutting iron, I think. Now listen to me, carefully. You know what a file is?'

'Yes, sir,' I answered.

'And food? Do you know what food is?'

'Yes, sir.'

'Then get me a file and some food. If you don't, I'll cut your heart out! Bring them to me early tomorrow morning. Come to that old building over there, down on the marshes. Don't tell anyone that you've seen me, and I'll not hurt you.'

'Yes, sir.'

'Now, don't think that I'm all on my own. There's a young man hiding in that building with me. He's far crueller than I am. Oh, he is cruel, that young man is! He has a secret way of finding out where boys are. A boy like you could never hide from him. Oh, no. A boy might lock his door and hide in his warm bed with the sheets pulled up over his head. A boy might think himself all comfortable and safe. But that young man will softly creep nearer and nearer and then jump on him and tear him open. When we saw you just now, that cruel young man wanted to hurt you. It was very hard for me to stop him. So what do you say? Will you bring me what I want?'

I promised to bring him the file and the food as he asked. 'Keep your promise, then,' he said. 'If you don't, you remember what I've told you about that young man! Now — go home.'

I ran home as fast as I could.

Joe and Mrs Joe

My sister was more than twenty years older than me, and she was not a good-looking woman. She was tall and thin with a red face and a very bad temper. Joe himself was a big, strong man, but he was kind and gentle. Joe and I were great friends. We were both very frightened of Mrs Joe.

When I got home from the churchyard, the forge was closed. I could not get the file. I went into our house, and found Joe sitting alone in the kitchen.

'Mrs Joe is looking for you outside, Pip,' he said sadly.

'Is she?' I asked.

'Yes, Pip, and she has got the stick with her.'

'Has she been gone a long time, Joe?'

'Well, she has been outside for about five minutes, Pip,' replied Joe. Then suddenly he said: 'She is coming! Quick, hide behind the door, Pip!'

I hid behind the door and my sister came in. She found me at once.

'Where have you been, you young dog?' she shouted. 'I've been worried sick about you!'

'I've only been to the churchyard,' I said.

'Churchyard!' shouted my sister. 'If I had not taken care of you, you would have been buried in the churchyard. You would have been dead long ago. There was no one else to take care of you. Remember that!'

I looked out towards the marshes. I thought of my prisoner, and the terrible young man, and the file, the food and the promise I had made.

Mrs Joe was putting our supper on the table. I sat beside Joe. He looked at me, and at his wife, and then looked down at the table. Joe was the strongest man I have ever known, but he was very afraid of my sister.

I was hungry, but I did not eat the bread that my sister had cut for me. I had to keep it for my prisoner and for his friend. There was not much food in the house that I could take without being found out. I decided to put my bread and butter in my pocket. Afterwards, I ran upstairs and hid it in my room.

Another escape

After supper, I sat beside the fire. It was a very cold night. Suddenly, we heard gunfire coming from very far away.

'Listen, Joe,' I asked, 'why are the guns firing?'

'It's to tell people that another prisoner has escaped,' Joe answered. 'A prisoner ran away last night, too. I heard the shots.'

I kept quiet for some time. Then I asked:

'Where do those shots come from?'

'From the prison-ships on the river, near the marshes,' my sister replied sharply. She did not like me to ask questions.

'Who are put into prison-ships? Why are they put there?'

'People are put into prison-ships because they kill other people, and they steal things from other people,' said my sister. 'They do all kinds of bad things. Bad people are always put into prison-ships. And bad people are always asking questions. So you stop asking questions and go to bed!'

The young man

The next morning, I woke up very early and went downstairs. I stole a pie, and wrapped it in a piece of cloth. Then I looked for something to give the prisoner to drink. There was a large, stone jar of brandy in the kitchen. I poured some into an empty bottle, and took that.

There was a door in the kitchen that led into the forge. I went through and took one of Joe's files. Then I ran to the marshes.

It was a wet, misty morning. The mist was so thick that I did not see the sign-post, pointing back to our village, until I was very near it. When I reached the marshes, it was even worse. It was so misty that I could not see my way.

I had often been to the old building on Sundays with Joe. I knew the place well. But because of the mist, I lost my way and I had to walk back along the riverside. I walked quickly. Suddenly I saw a man sitting in front of me, his arms folded as if he was asleep. His back was towards me. I thought it was my prisoner so I went up softly and touched him on the shoulder. He jumped to his feet at once, and turned round.

He was not the man I had met.

He was also dressed in rough, grey clothes and had a chain on his leg like my prisoner. But on the side of his face was a deep cut.

The stranger gave a terrible cry and tried to hit me. But he must have been very weak, because he missed me and almost fell down. Then he ran away into the mist.

'It's the young man!' I thought, and trembled.

I ran to the building, and found my prisoner waiting. I gave him the file and he put it down on the grass. Then he seized the food I gave him and ate it as if he was dying from hunger.

I feel sorry for the prisoner

'What is in the bottle, boy?' he asked.

'Brandy,' I replied.

He stopped eating and drank some of the brandy. He was shaking because of the cold and could not hold the bottle still while he was drinking.

'I think you are ill,' I said.

'I think I am, boy.'

'It's very wet around here,' I told him. 'You shouldn't have been lying on the wet ground.'

'Well then, I'll eat my breakfast before I die of the cold. If they were going to hang me, I would still want to eat my breakfast first, that's the truth!' 5

He ate very fast. Then suddenly he stopped eating. He looked around quickly, like a dog that has heard something suspicious.

'Have you brought anyone with you?' he asked. 10

'No, sir, no!' I cried.

'Well, I believe you,' he said. 'You're too young to take pleasure in seeing a poor prisoner caught by the soldiers. I don't think you would bring soldiers to hunt for me.' 15

I felt sorry for him. Watching him eat the pie, I said: 'I'm glad you are enjoying it.'

'Thank you, my boy.'

The other prisoner

After a while, I asked: 20

'Aren't you giving any of the pie to your friend?'

He stopped eating: 'My friend?' he asked.

'To the young man, the one you talked about yesterday,' I told him.

'Oh, him!' he said and laughed. 'He doesn't want any 25 food.'

'But he looked very hungry, sir!' I said.

The man stopped eating. He stared at me.

'Looked? You mean you saw him? When?' he asked.

'Just now.' 30

'Where?'

'Over there,' I pointed. 'I found him asleep. I thought it was you.'

He caught hold of me and shook me.

'What did he look like? Quick, boy!'

'He was dressed like you. And he had a chain on his leg too. Didn't you hear the gun shots last night?'

5   'So there were shots last night,' he said to himself. 'That means that somebody else has escaped from the prison-ship.'

The prisoner tries to free himself

Then he turned to me and asked:

10   'What about his face, Pip? Was there anything strange about his face?'

'There was a cut on it, on the left side.'

'Aha! Where is he now? Show me the way he went.' He put the remaining food inside his coat.

15   I pointed in the direction where the other man had gone.

He stared into the mist. Then he took the file and started to rub it against the chain on his leg to cut it free. He did not pay any attention to me, so I decided 20   to go.

The last I saw of him, he was sitting there in the mist. He was bent over, working hard with the file as he tried to cut through the chain. I walked a little way then stopped and looked back. He was hidden by the mist 25   and I could not see him. But I could still hear the sound made by the file on the chain.

CHRISTMAS DAY

Guests

The day when I took food to the prisoner was Christmas Day. A few people were coming to our house for Christmas dinner. They were Mr and Mrs Hubble, Uncle Pumblechook, and Mr Wopsle. Mr Wopsle was the ⁵ priest's helper at our church. The dinner was at half-past one.

Joe and I went to church. When we got home, the table had already been set. Everything was ready.

My job was to open the door for our guests. The first ¹⁰ to arrive was Mr Wopsle, then Mr and Mrs Hubble. The last one was Uncle Pumblechook.

'Mrs Joe,' said Uncle Pumblechook, 'I have brought you two bottles of wine!'

Every Christmas Day, Uncle Pumblechook brought ¹⁵ two bottles of wine for my sister. And every year, she would say: 'Oh Uncle Pumblechook, how kind!'

After dinner, everyone sat around the table and talked. Uncle Pumblechook talked about little boys and how bad they were. Then he talked about how little ²⁰ boys should be grateful to their sisters who looked after them.

'Dear Uncle, how right you are!' cried my sister. 'Will you have a little brandy?'

I trembled when I heard this. I had taken some ²⁵ brandy from the large stone bottle to give to the prisoner. To make the bottle full again, I had poured in some water. When Uncle Pumblechook drank the brandy, he would know that it had water in it. Then my sister would know that I had taken some! ³⁰

Trouble for Pip

My sister went to get the brandy and poured a glass for
Uncle Pumblechook. He held up his glass to the light,
looked at it carefully, and smiled. Holding his head
5   back, he drank it all at once.

Then a terrible thing happened. Uncle Pumblechook
suddenly began to cough and
hold his throat. My sister
and Joe ran to him. I was
so terrified that I could
not move. I thought
I had killed Uncle
Pumblechook.

Uncle Pumblechook
fell back in his chair,
looking very sick, and
whispered:

'Medicine! There is medicine
in that brandy!'

'Medicine?' cried my sister.
'How did medicine get into
the bottle?'

Only I knew the answer. My sister had said she was
going to make some medicine to give to me. She must
25   have made it in the water jug. When I filled the stone
bottle from the jug, I had put medicine in by mistake.
I knew that my sister's medicine had a very unpleasant
taste. It also had a very unpleasant effect. I knew Uncle
Pumblechook would feel even sicker later on.

30   But Uncle Pumblechook did not wait for an answer.
He asked for hot gin and water. My sister immediately
went to get it for him. She was so busy taking care of
Uncle Pumblechook, she forgot all about the medicine
in the brandy.

After some time, I stopped trembling. Uncle Pumblechook was enjoying his gin and water. I thought I was safe. Then my sister said to Joe: 'Bring some clean plates, Joe!'

Suddenly I knew what was going to happen.   5

'Uncle Pumblechook has given us such a nice present,' said my sister. 'He sent it here yesterday. It's a pork pie. You shall all have a piece!'

She went into another room to get the pie. And I had given the pie to the prisoner!   10

Uncle Pumblechook was licking his lips. I heard Joe say: 'You shall have some pie too, Pip.'

I was very frightened.

My sister would find out this time. I would be punished. I decided I had better get away! I got up from   15
my chair, and ran.

When I reached the door, it opened. There, standing outside, was a group of soldiers. One of them held out a pair of handcuffs to me. He said:

'Here you are, be quick, come on!'   20

A job for Joe

When they heard the soldiers, all the guests and Joe went quickly to the door. My sister came back into the room. She did not have the pie with her. She stopped and looked at everybody, and said: 'Where is the pie?'   25

The officer and I were standing in the room. It was he who had spoken to me before. He was looking at everybody. His left hand was on my shoulder. He held the handcuffs in his other hand.

'Excuse me, ladies and gentlemen,' he said, 'we're the   30
King's soldiers. We're on our way to look for two escaped prisoners, and we need the blacksmith.'

'What for?' asked my sister.

'Madam,' said the officer, 'we want him to do a bit of work for the King's soldiers.'

Turning to Joe, he went on, 'You see, blacksmith, one of these handcuffs is broken, and we have to use them
5   now. Can you fix them?'

Joe looked at the handcuffs and said, 'I'll have to light my fire. The work will take some time.'

'Will it? Then you begin at once, blacksmith,' said the officer. 'My men will help you.'

10   After hearing all this, I felt a lot better. The soldiers had saved me. They had made my sister forget about the pie. She was too surprised to do anything.

'Sorry to interrupt your Christmas dinner,' continued the officer, 'but we must get to the marshes before
15   sunset. We believe that the escaped prisoners are there. They won't try to leave the marshes before dark. Has anybody here seen them?'

Everybody, except me, said no.

'Well,' said the officer, 'they'll be caught before very
20   long. Now, blacksmith, are you ready?'

Joe went into the forge and picked up his hammer. One of the soldiers lit the fire. It was soon burning brightly. Then Joe began to work.

Two hours later, his work was done.

Joe and Mr Wopsle decided to go with the soldiers to watch them searching for the prisoners. Joe asked my sister if I could go with them.

'If that boy gets shot, don't ask me to look after him!' she replied. This meant that I could go.

We started off for the marshes.

The soldiers told Mr Wopsle, Joe and me to walk behind them. We had to keep quiet. On the way, I said to Joe softly: 'I hope the soldiers don't find the prisoners.'

'Let's hope the poor men have already gone, Pip,' Joe replied.

The soldiers stopped walking when we reached the churchyard. Two or three of them looked among the graves for the prisoners. They did not find anything and came back. Then we went towards the marshes.

The east wind blew the rain on our faces. It was very cold. Joe carried me on his back. I looked all round for the prisoners. I could not see or hear anything.

Suddenly the soldiers stopped walking. They had heard something. But it was only the sound of a sheep. The sheep stopped eating and looked at us. There was nothing else to be heard.

My prisoner and the young man

The soldiers were moving towards the old building. We were walking a little way behind them. Suddenly we all stopped. We could hear shouting!

As we went nearer, we could hear that the shouting was made by more than one person. The soldiers ran quickly towards the noise. We ran after them.

A voice called out: 'Help!' Another shouted, 'We're here! The escaped prisoners are here!'

The soldiers ran very fast. Joe ran after them, carrying me on his back. In front of us we could see two men fighting each other.

'Here they are! Both of them!' cried the officer. 'You can't escape now, you two! Stop fighting! Get up, get up!'

The soldiers rushed forward and separated the two prisoners. I saw that one of them was my prisoner, the one I had helped. The other was the terrible young man.

'I caught him!' shouted my prisoner. 'I caught him for you. Don't forget that!'

'That won't do you any good,' said the officer. 'You're an escaped prisoner yourself.'

'I don't want anything,' said my prisoner. 'I caught him. He knows it. That's good enough for me.'

The other prisoner seemed to be badly hurt. He could hardly speak. He was leaning on a soldier to stop himself from falling.

Handcuffs were put on both prisoners.

'Guard, please know that he tried to kill me,' said the other prisoner.

'Tried to kill him!' said my prisoner. 'If I'd wanted to kill him, he would have been dead long ago. I caught him and gave him to you. That's what I did! Why should I kill him? It would be doing him a good deed. I can do a worse thing to him. I caught him and gave him to you.'

The other prisoner said again: 'He tried … he tried to kill me!'

'He lies!' shouted my prisoner. 'He was telling lies when he was born, and he'll still be telling lies when he dies! Look at his face. You can see that he tells lies. Let him look me in the face. He can't do it, because he tells lies!'

The other man did not look at my prisoner's face. He looked at the soldiers, he looked at the sky. He looked at everything except the face of my prisoner. He was shaking with fear.

Then my prisoner looked around and saw me for the first time. I had got down from Joe's back, and had not moved since. I wanted him to know that I was still his friend and that I did not want him to be caught. But he stared at me in a strange way. Then he looked away again.

Inside the wooden hut

The soldiers began to march to the prison-ships on the river. Mr Wopsle, Joe and I followed. The two prisoners were kept apart. Each of them was guarded by a group of soldiers. I held Joe's hand.

After about an hour of walking, we came to a wooden hut by the river. We went in. Inside there was a bright fire, a lamp, some guns and a low bed. The officer wrote something in a book. Then the other prisoner was taken first to the prison-ship in a small boat.

My prisoner did not look at me again. While we were in the hut, he stood in front of the fire, thinking. Suddenly he turned to the officer and said: 'I wish to say something about this escape. I don't want other people to get into trouble because of me. I stole some food in the village beyond the marshes, from the blacksmith's house.'

'Well!' said the officer, looking at Joe.

'Well, Pip!' said Joe, looking at me. They were both very surprised.

'It was some bread ... that's what it was ... and brandy and a pie ...'

'Was any pie stolen from your house, blacksmith?' the officer asked Joe quietly.

Joe nodded. 'Yes, my wife learnt about it when you came in.'

'So,' said my prisoner, looking at Joe, 'you are the blacksmith, are you? Then I'm sorry to say, I've eaten your pie.'

'I'm glad you had it,' said Joe. 'We don't know what you've done. But we wouldn't like you to die of hunger, poor man, would we, Pip?'

My prisoner made a strange sound in his throat and turned his back on us. The boat had returned, and his guards were ready. He was put into the boat.

By the light of the guards' torches, we could see the black prison-ship a little way from the shore. We saw the boat reach the prison-ship. Then my prisoner was taken up the side of the ship. After that, we could not see him any more.

The torches were thrown into the water, and it was suddenly very dark. Joe put me on his back, and carried me all the way home.

MISS HAVISHAM

A rich old lady

A year passed. Then, one cold evening, Mrs Joe came home from a day at the market looking very excited. With her was Uncle Pumblechook, who was rubbing his hands together and looking important. I was sitting with Joe next to the fire. We stared at each other in surprise.

'Now,' said Mrs Joe, 'I hope the boy will be thankful tonight. If he is not, he's a very ungrateful young dog.'

I tried to look thankful, though I did not know why I should.

'I hope,' said my sister, 'she'll not spoil him.'

'I'm sure she'll not spoil him, madam,' said Uncle Pumblechook. Joe and I continued to stare at each other. What were my sister and Uncle Pumblechook talking about? My sister saw our puzzled faces.

'What's the matter with you two?'

'Well,' said Joe carefully, 'you were talking about a "she". Who … um …?'

'Idiot! What else is Miss Havisham but a "she"?' interrupted Mrs Joe. 'You can't call her a "he", can you?'

'I have heard of a Miss Havisham who lives in the town …' Joe continued, even more carefully.

'Is there any other Miss Havisham?' shouted my sister, her angry face redder than ever. 'She told Uncle Pumblechook that she wants a boy to go to her house, and play there. Uncle Pumblechook thought of Pip, and of course, I am letting Pip go. And he had better play there, or he'll be in trouble!'

I had heard of Miss Havisham. She lived in a large, dark house, which she never left.

'Miss Havisham is a rich and lonely old lady, Joe,' said Uncle Pumblechook. 'Some good might come of this.'

'Joseph,' cried my sister, 'see how much Uncle Pumblechook cares about Pip's future! Who knows what might happen if Miss Havisham becomes fond of Pip! Tonight Pip will stay in Uncle Pumblechook's house. Tomorrow morning, Uncle Pumblechook will take him to see Miss Havisham.'

Miss Havisham

Uncle Pumblechook took me to Miss Havisham's house at ten o'clock the next morning. We rang the gate-bell and waited.

A window opened and a clear voice asked: 'What name?'

'Pumblechook!'

'Quite right!' said the voice, and the window banged shut again. A young lady then came across the yard, holding some keys in her hand.

'This,' said Uncle Pumblechook, 'is Pip.'

'This is Pip, is it?' said the young lady. She was very pretty, and seemed very proud. 'Come in, Pip.'

Uncle Pumblechook also wanted to come in, but she stopped him, so he had to leave me there.

We went into the house by a side door. The passage was dark. The girl had left a lighted candle there. She took it up and we went through more passages. Then we went up the stairs. It was still very dark.

At last, we came to the door of a room. The girl asked me to go in, and then she walked away, taking the candle with her. I was left alone in the dark.

Trembling, I knocked at the door.

'Come in!'

I went in, and found myself in a large room, lit by candles. All the curtains were drawn. There was no daylight.

Then I saw her — the strangest lady I had ever seen. She was sitting in a large chair, her head resting on her hand. She was dressed all in white, from her head to her toes. Even her hair was white, and on top of it she wore a long white veil. She wore only one shoe. The other was on the floor.

'Who is it?' she asked.

'Pip,' I replied shyly. 'I have come to play.'

'Come nearer. Let me look at you. Come closer. Do I look strange to you? Well, I have not gone out of this house for many years. I have not seen the sun since you were born. Are you afraid of me?'

I said, 'No,' but it was a lie. I was afraid of her.

'Do you know what I am touching, here?' she asked suddenly. She touched the left side of her chest.

'Yes, madam, your heart,' I replied.

'It's broken!' she cried. 'But now, I want to see someone play. Play! Play!'

'He's very common'

But I did not know what to do. I stood looking at her.

'You rude little boy!' she said. 'I asked you to play.'

'Madam, I am very sorry but I cannot,' I replied. 'I
5   would like to, but everything is so strange here, and so sad …'

Then I stopped. I was afraid I had said too much.

Miss Havisham was staring at herself in the mirror. She did not seem to have heard me.

10 After some time, she said: 'Call Estella. You can do that, I'm sure. Go to her room and call her.'

I did not like to do this. The house was so strange, and the passage was so dark. But after I had called three or four times, Estella came.

15 Miss Havisham asked her to come near and said: 'Let me see you play cards with this boy.'

We sat down to play cards. Before our first game was finished, Estella said nastily:

'What rough hands he has! And what thick boots! He
20 doesn't have good manners either. He's very common.'

I did not like her to make fun of my hands and boots and I did not like to be called common. I felt my face grow red.

'What do you think of her?' Miss Havisham asked me.

25 'I think she's very pretty,' I replied slowly.

'Anything else?'

'I think she's very proud. And very rude.'

'Anything else?'

'I think I want to go home.'

30 'Don't you want to come and see her again?' asked Miss Havisham. 'She's so pretty.'

'Maybe,' I said. 'But I want to go home now.'

'You shall go soon,' she said, 'but finish the game first.'

I am unhappy

Estella and I played the game until we finished. When she won, she threw all the cards on the table. She said she did not care whether she won or lost. Then Miss Havisham asked her to take me away and give me 5 something to eat. She told me to come back to see her again after six days.

Estella took me out of the house, and I was left alone in the yard. I looked at my hands and boots. They were rough and thick. I knew then that Estella was right, and 10 that I was common. I had never thought about it before. But after what Estella had said, I felt very troubled. I blamed Joe for my rough hands and thick boots. And I wished he had good manners. Then I would have learnt good manners from him. 15

Estella came with some bread and meat for me. She put the food down on the ground as if I was a dog. She didn't even look at me. Tears came to my eyes. She saw them and smiled. Then she left me.

When she was gone, I hid behind one of the gates and cried. I kicked the wall with helpless anger. After doing that I felt better.

When I had finished eating, I looked around the house. I was alone. At the farthest end of the yard, there was a high wall. I climbed up the wall and looked over it. On the other side was a garden, filled with long grass. Then Estella came with the keys to let me out.

She opened the gate and stood holding it. I walked towards it without looking at her. But when I reached the gate, she touched my arm and asked: 'Why don't you cry?'

5 'Because I don't want to!'

'You do,' she laughed. 'You've been crying so much you can hardly see. You're nearly crying again now.'

Then she pushed me through the gate and locked it. I walked home feeling very unhappy.

10 My second visit

After six days, I went to Miss Havisham's house again. I rang the bell at the gate, and Estella came to let me in. She led me to a different part of the house.

'You must come this way today,' she said.

15 We went into a dark room on the ground floor at the back of the house. There were some visitors in the room. Estella told me to go and stand by the window. I did as she told me, but I felt very uncomfortable. I thought that the visitors must all be looking at me.

20 They stopped talking when I came into the room. But after a while, they began speaking again, taking no notice of me.

A bell rang, and someone called out in the passage. The visitors stopped talking and Estella said to me:

25 'Now, boy. We must go to Miss Havisham's room.'

They all looked at me. As I went out, one of them said:

'Well, I don't know what to say! What will happen next?'

30 Someone replied: 'Who could have imagined this?'

As Estella led me into the dark passage with a candle, she stopped suddenly and put her face was very close to mine. She asked: 'Well?'

I did not know what I should say.

'Am I pretty?' she asked suddenly.

'Yes, you are,' I replied.

'Am I unkind?'

'Not so much as you were the last time.'   5

'Not so much?'

'No.'

She hit me angrily. 'What do you think of me now?'

'I shan't tell you.'

'Why not?' she asked. 'Are you going to tell   10
Miss Havisham? Is that why you won't tell me?'

'No,' I said.

'Why don't you cry again, boy?'

'Because I'll never cry for you again,' I shouted.

But this was not true. Inside, I was crying for her   15
then. I would go on crying for her for many years.

The wedding cake

We went on our way. As we were going up the stairs,
we met a gentleman coming down.

'Who is this?' he asked, stopping and looking at me.   20

'A boy,' said Estella.

He was a big, dark, fierce-looking man.

'You live near here, do you?' he asked me.

'Yes, sir.'

'What are you doing here?'   25

'Miss Havisham asked me to come, sir.'

'Well, behave yourself! I know many things about
boys. Bad things. So you behave yourself!'

After saying this, he let me go and went on his way.
I was very glad when he left me.   30

I did not have much time to think about him. Soon
I was in Miss Havisham's room. Both she and the room
looked exactly the same as the last time I was there.

Miss Havisham was looking at the table. I stood at the door for some time. Then she turned around to look at me.

'So,' she said, 'it's time for your visit again. Are you ready to play?'

'No, madam.'

'Very well, then,' she said, 'since you are not willing to play, are you willing to work?'

I nodded violently. 'Yes!'

'Then go into the opposite room and wait there until I come,' she said.

I did so. The room was very dark. Everything in it was very old and covered with dust. In the middle of the room was a long table with a cloth on it. It looked as if it had been made ready for a party with a lot of guests. But there were spiders' webs on the plates and glasses.

I was staring at all these things when Miss Havisham came in. She put her hand on my shoulder. Then she pointed her stick at what looked like a large pile of spiders' webs in the middle of the table.

'What do you think that is, Pip?' she whispered.

'I don't know, madam.'

'It's a cake. My wedding cake!' She leaned heavily on my shoulder. 'Now walk with me, boy. Help me to walk!'

The visitors

That was my work. I had to help Miss Havisham walk round and round the room. She leaned on my shoulder, and we walked round and round the room together.

After a while, she said, 'Call Estella!'   5

So I went into the passage and called Estella. When I saw her candle-light coming towards me, I went back. Miss Havisham and I began to walk round the room again.

Estella brought some people with her. They were the   10
three ladies and the gentleman I had seen before. I felt very uncomfortable. I did not know what to do. I wanted to stop walking with Miss Havisham. But she made me go on.

Estella went away again. The three ladies stood in a   15
corner of the room. Miss Havisham did not look at them at all. After a while, they began to talk to each other.

'It's strange that Matthew never visits Miss Havisham,' said one of the ladies.

When she heard this, Miss Havisham stopped   20
walking. She turned to face the lady who had spoken.

'Matthew Pocket will come to see me only when I am dead,' she said. And then she turned to me: 'Walk with me, walk with me!' I continued my work.

After some time, Estella came back. Then   25
Miss Havisham said, 'Let me see you two play cards. Be quick!'

Joe's Apprentice

The fight

Estella and I went back to Miss Havisham's room. We sat down to play cards. I lost again. We played five or six games, and all the time, Miss Havisham watched us.

5   Then I was told what day I was to come again. I was taken down into the yard, given some food and left alone as before. After I had eaten, I began to look around.

    I thought the visitors had left and the house was now
10 empty, so I looked in at a window. To my surprise, I saw a pale young gentleman inside. He was watching me. He was not much older than me. He quickly came out.

    'Hello, young man!' he said. 'Who let you in?'
15   'Miss Estella,' I replied.

    'And who told you that you can walk about in here?'

    'Miss Estella.'

    'Come and fight,' he said. 'But wait a minute. I must give you a reason for fighting.'

20   Then he pulled my hair and hit me.

    'Now you have a reason for fighting,' he said. 'But let's go to another place before we begin. We must get everything ready first.'

    I followed him to the end of the garden. Then he
25 went away and got a bottle of water and a piece of wet cloth.

    'This will be enough for both of us,' he said, and took off his coat.

We began our fight. I hit
him first. To my surprise, he
fell down on his back. His
nose was bleeding.

He got up and rubbed his face
with the wet cloth. Then he came back to me.

We started hitting at each other. He was soon
out of breath. Then I hit him hard in the eye,
and again he fell down on his back.

I was surprised that I had beaten him so easily.
He looked so young and brave. Although he had started
the fight, I felt very sorry for him. I put my coat back
on and asked: 'Can I help you?'

'No, thank you,' he replied.

'Well, goodbye.'   15

'Goodbye to you, too.'

Then I went back to the yard. Estella was waiting for
me with the gate-keys.

My future

I was worried about the fight with the pale young   20
gentleman. I thought I would be punished. For some
days I stayed at home, afraid that a policeman would
come looking for me.

The day came when I had to go to Miss Havisham's
house again. But when I reached the house, nothing   25
was said about the fight and I didn't see the pale young
gentleman.

Miss Havisham had begun to talk more to me. She asked me what I had learnt, and what I was going to do when I was older. I told her that I was going to be Joe's apprentice. I was going to learn how to be a blacksmith. I also told her that I was very eager to learn, but now I knew very little.

I had hoped that she would help me. But she did not say anything. She did not give me any money or anything else except my dinner.

At home, my sister and Mr Pumblechook talked about what Miss Havisham would do for me. They hoped that she would give me a lot of money so that I could be a gentleman. Then I would not have to become a blacksmith. I would not need to work at all.

Joe did not join in their talking. He did not want me to leave the forge. He wanted me to work with him. This always made my sister very angry, and in the end she would shout at me:

'You young dog, we're tired of you! Go to bed. You have given us enough trouble for one night!'

This happened many times.

Miss Havisham asks for Joe

One day, Miss Havisham and I were walking together round her room. Suddenly, she stopped and said: 'Pip, you're growing tall! Tell me again the name of your blacksmith.'

'Joe Gargery, madam.'

'He'll be your master soon, then. You're going to become his apprentice, aren't you?'

'Yes, Miss Havisham.'

'Then you'd better become an apprentice at once,' she said. 'Ask Joe Gargery to come here with you. Tell him to bring any papers that need to be signed.'

Two days later, Joe put on his best clothes to go with me to Miss Havisham's house. Estella opened the gate for us. When Joe saw her, he took off his hat and held it tightly in his hands. He looked very uncomfortable.

Estella led us through the dark passages of the house   5
to Miss Havisham's room. I took Joe by the arm and led him. Miss Havisham was sitting at her table, and she turned around to look at us.

'Ah!' she said to Joe. 'So you are the husband of this boy's sister? And you hope to make him your   10
apprentice? Is that so, Mr Gargery?'

Joe was too frightened, and too shy to speak to Miss Havisham. He was so uncomfortable that he spoke to me instead, as if I was asking the questions. I felt very ashamed of him.   15

'You know, Pip,' he said, 'that you and I are the best of friends. And I'd like you to help me at the forge. But, Pip, if you don't want to be a blacksmith, please tell me. I'll see what we can do for you.'

Miss Havisham asked: 'Has the boy said that he   20
doesn't want to be a blacksmith?'

'You know, Pip,' Joe said to me, 'you always said you wanted to be a blacksmith.'

'Have you brought the papers that have to be signed?' asked Miss Havisham.   25

'Well, Pip,' said Joe, 'you saw me put the papers into my hat. Therefore, you know that I have brought the papers with me.'

Then he took the papers from his hat and gave them to me.   30

Joe is my master

I looked up and saw Estella standing behind Miss Havisham's chair, laughing at Joe. I hated myself

for feeling ashamed of dear Joe at that moment, but I could not help it.

I took the papers from him and gave them to Miss Havisham. She read them and then said to Joe: 'You do not want any money for teaching Pip to become a blacksmith?'

Joe did not reply.

'Joe,' I said, 'why don't you answer?'

'Pip,' he said, 'you know that we don't talk about money between us. You know that I don't want money for teaching you to become a blacksmith. Therefore, you know the answer to that question is "No". So do I have to say it?'

Miss Havisham took a little bag from the table beside her.

'I must pay Pip for the work he has done here,' she said. 'There are twenty-five pounds in this bag. Give the money to your master, Pip.'

'This is very kind of you, Pip,' Joe said. 'The money will be very useful. But I should not have asked for it.'

'Goodbye, Pip!' said Miss Havisham. 'Let them out, Estella.'

'Am I to come again, Miss Havisham?' I asked.

'No, Gargery is your master now,' she replied. Then she said to Joe: 'Gargery, I want to say something to you. Pip has been a good boy here. The money is to pay for his work. And it has been paid to you because you're going to teach him. And, Mr Gargery, you should not expect any more money from me.'

Soon after that Joe and I were outside the gate. Estella shut it. Then she was gone.

A holiday

I was never very happy at home. My sister was always
unkind to me. Our house was rough and poor, and I
was ashamed of it. I would not have liked
Miss Havisham or Estella to see it.   5

I had always thought I would be happy when I was
Joe's apprentice, but I was not. I did not want to be a
blacksmith any more. But I am glad that I did not tell
Joe this. It would have made him so sad.

Joe had another helper in the forge. His name was   10
Orlick, and he was very strong. He was also a very
unpleasant man, who did not like anybody, and nobody
liked him. He disliked me very much.

One day, I asked Joe to let me have a holiday. I told
him I wanted to see Miss Havisham. The truth is that I   15
wanted to see Estella.

Orlick was also working in the forge. He did not say
anything then. But later on, Orlick said: 'Now, master,
if you give him a holiday, you must give Old Orlick a
holiday too.' (He always called himself Old Orlick,   20
although he was only about twenty-five years old.)

'Why?' Joe asked. 'What are you going to do?'

'What am I going to do? What is he going to do?'
shouted Orlick. 'I've as many things to do as he has.'

'Pip is going to town,' said Joe.   25

'If he is going to town, then Old Orlick is going to
town as well. Both of us can go to town. Now, master,
give me a holiday.'

'Well,' said Joe thoughtfully, 'you've been doing well
at your work. Let's all have a holiday!'   30

All this while, my sister had been standing outside
the forge. She could hear everything that was said. At
once, she looked in at a window, and said to Joe: 'Idiot!
Why should you give holidays to men like him? Do you

want to pay him money for not working? You must be a rich man! If I was his master, I wouldn't give him any holiday at all.'

Orlick was very angry at this and he called Mrs Joe some terrible names. Joe tried to make Orlick stop, but Orlick would not. Mrs Joe was nearly mad with anger. Joe had to stop Orlick. So he hit him.

Joe was a very strong man. I had never seen anybody knock him down. Orlick was also very strong, but he could not fight Joe. He fell down onto the floor, and could hardly get up.

After that, I went into the house and put on my best clothes to go to town. When I went back to the forge, Joe and Orlick were drinking beer together. They had forgotten about the fight and were friends again.

Estella has gone away

When I reached town, I went straight to Miss Havisham's house. I was very nervous. Miss Havisham had not invited me to the house, and I did not have any reason to see her. I came only because I wanted to see Estella.

Inside the house I found everything the same. Miss Havisham was alone.

'Well,' she said, 'what have you come for? Do you want anything?'

'No, Miss Havisham,' I replied. 'I wanted you to know that I am doing well in my work. I'm very grateful to you.'

I wondered where Estella was. I looked around for her, but I could not see her.

'I hope Estella is well,' I said at last.

'She's not here,' said Miss Havisham. 'She's abroad, learning how to be a lady. She's far away, prettier than

ever, and loved by all who see her. Do you feel that
you've lost her, Pip?'

I did not know what to say. Miss Havisham soon sent
me away. When the gate closed behind me, I felt even
more unhappy with my home and my work. That was   5
all I got from going to see Miss Havisham.

I met Mr Wopsle in town, and went with him to see
Uncle Pumblechook. It was very dark when we started
to walk home. Halfway there we met someone sitting
by the roadside.   10

'Hallo!' said Mr Wopsle. 'Is that Orlick?'

'Yes,' said the man. 'I was waiting for you. I don't
want to walk back alone.'

We all walked on together. At last, we came to the
village. Something seemed to have happened. There   15
were a lot of people standing about with lamps, looking
very excited.

Mr Wopsle went to ask what had happened, and then
ran back to us.

'There's something wrong at your house, Pip. We   20
must hurry!' he shouted.

We all began to run, and did not stop until we
reached the house. I went straight into the kitchen.

Joe was there. There was also a doctor, a policeman,
and some women. They moved back to let me pass   25
through. Then I saw my sister lying on the ground.

She had been hit on the back of the head.

For many years, we did not know who had done
this.

BIDDY

Biddy comes to the forge

My sister did not die, but she was never the same again. She could not see or speak clearly, and she was very weak. She sat quietly by the fire all day. She was never angry.

Mr Wopsle's niece, Biddy, came to take care of her. When I was a little boy, Biddy had taught me to read and write. She now took care of my sister as if she was a little child.

Joe was very unhappy about what had happened to his wife. She had not been pretty or kind, but he had loved her. However, life at the forge was much more pleasant after Mrs Joe was attacked.

I worked in the forge day after day, and I hated it more and more. Every year on my birthday, I visited Miss Havisham. Estella was never there. It was Estella who had made me hate my work. She had made me ashamed of my home.

One evening I was practising my writing. I had always wanted to read and write properly like Estella. While I was writing, I noticed Biddy's eyes. They were pretty eyes, and wise. She was watching me. I stopped and put down my pen.

'Biddy,' I asked, 'how do you manage to learn everything that I have learnt? Every day I am learning new things. Yet, you already know everything that I learn.'

'Perhaps,' she replied, 'it is because I like learning. I find it easy to learn. I was your first teacher, you know.'

'Yes, Biddy, you were my first teacher. When you were teaching me, I never thought that this would happen. I never thought that my sister would be ill, and you would be taking her place. I never thought that we would be together like this.'

'Ah, poor thing!' replied Biddy. She was thinking of my sister.

'Biddy,' I said, 'let's go for a walk on the marshes. I want to have a long talk with you.'

'I want to be a gentleman'

Biddy and I walked along together on the marshes. It was a beautiful day.

We sat down by the river.

'Biddy, you must promise me this. You must never tell anybody what I'm going to tell you now.'

'I promise, Pip.'

'I want to be a gentleman. I don't want to be a blacksmith,' I said.

'Oh, Pip, are you sure?' she said sadly. 'You know best what is good for you. But aren't you happy now, as Joe's apprentice?'

'Biddy,' I said, 'I'm not at all happy as I am. I don't like my work, and I don't like my life. I can only be happy when I become a gentleman. I wouldn't mind being a blacksmith. But somebody said I was common. She laughed at me for wanting to be a blacksmith.'

Biddy looked at me. 'That was very unkind. Who did that?'

'The young lady at Miss Havisham's house,' I replied. 'She is more beautiful than anybody I have ever seen. I want to be a gentleman because of her.'

After a while, Biddy asked: 'Do you want to be a gentleman to make her angry? Is it because you want to show her that she was wrong? Or do you want to become a gentleman to please her?'

'I don't know,' I said.

Biddy continued: 'Well, I'll tell you my opinion. If you want to make her angry, then don't become a gentleman. Forget what she said. Don't care anything for her. And if you want to please her, don't waste your time. She laughed at you. She doesn't deserve to be pleased.'

'Perhaps you are right, Biddy,' I cried. 'But I cannot forget her.'

Biddy was a wise girl. She did not say anything. She did not want to hurt me.

'Biddy, I'll always tell you everything,' I said at last.

'Until you become a gentleman, Pip,' she said. 'You'll tell me everything until you become a gentleman. Then you won't tell me anything after that. Now, shall we go on walking? Or shall we go home?'

We walked a little further. Then we saw Orlick.

'Hallo!' he said. 'Where are you two going?'

'Where else can we be going?' I replied. 'We are going home.'

'Well, then,' he said. 'I'm going home with you.'

Biddy then said quietly to me: 'Don't let him come with us. I don't like him.'

I was quite happy to do as she asked. I told Orlick: 'Thank you, but you don't have to walk with us. We can get home without you.'

Orlick laughed nastily. He let us go on first, and followed a little way behind.

I had often thought it was Orlick that had attacked my sister. I wondered if Biddy thought the same thing.

'Why do you dislike Orlick?' I asked her.

'Because I am afraid he likes me,' she said.

After that day, I watched Orlick even more carefully.

A strange gentleman

I had been working as Joe's apprentice for more than three years. One Saturday night, Joe and I and a few friends were sitting beside the fire in the inn, when I noticed a strange gentleman. He seemed to be listening to our conversation. Suddenly he came over to us and looked at each of us carefully.

'I believe there is a blacksmith among you,' he said. 'His name is Joseph, or Joe, Gargery. Which is the man?'

'I am the man,' said Joe.

'You have an apprentice,' said the stranger. 'His name is Pip. Is he here?'

'I am here,' I replied.

The stranger did not know me, but I knew him. He was the big, dark man I met on the stairs in Miss Havisham's house.

'I wish to talk to you and Mr Gargery alone,' he said. 'It will take some time. We'd better go to your house.'

When we got home, the stranger sat down at the table.

'My name is Jaggers,' he said. 'I am a lawyer in London. I have some business to do with you. I am doing it for someone else. Mr Gargery, this person would like to take Mr Pip from you. Would you let
5 Mr Pip go if he asked you? This person is doing it for Mr Pip's good. Do you want money for letting Mr Pip go?'

'Of course I don't want anything for letting Pip go,' said Joe, staring. 'I'll let him go if it's for his own good.'

10 'Very well,' said Mr Jaggers. 'Now, this is what I have to tell you. Mr Pip has great expectations: many good things are going to happen to him.'

Joe and I looked at each other in surprise.

'Mr Pip will soon become very rich,' Mr Jaggers
15 continued. 'He will inherit a large fortune. However, the person who is giving Mr Pip the fortune wants him to leave the forge. He wants Mr Pip to become a gentleman.'

My dream had come true! The unknown person must be Miss Havisham. She was going to make me a very rich gentleman.

'Mr Pip,' said the lawyer, 'you must not know who the person is. Don't try to find out. When the time comes, you'll be told this person's name. Do you agree to this? If you do not, you must say so now. What have you to say?' I agreed.

Joe is surprised

'Mr Pip, you must learn to be a gentleman. You must have a gentleman's manners, and a gentleman's education. I know someone who can teach you,' said Mr Jaggers. 'His name is Mr Matthew Pocket.'   5

I remembered the name at once. I had heard it at Miss Havisham's house. One of the visitors had said: 'It's strange that Matthew never visits Miss Havisham.' Miss Havisham had replied: 'Matthew Pocket will come to see me only when I'm dead.'   10

'I've heard the name before,' I said.

'Well then,' said Jaggers, 'how would you like to study under him?'

I said that I would be glad to do so.

'Good. I'll tell him to expect you. You'll meet his son   15
too. The son lives in London. When will you come to London?'

Joe was staring at the two of us. I said: 'I think I can come at once.'

'No, no,' said Mr Jaggers. 'First you must have some   20
new clothes. Come to London in a week's time. You'll want some money. I'll give you twenty pounds.' Then he said to Joe: 'Well, Joseph Gargery, you look very surprised.'

'I am,' said Joe.   25

'You've said you don't want anything,' said Mr Jaggers. 'But I'll pay you some money, as you're losing Pip's help in the forge.'

Joe put his hand on my shoulder. 'I'm glad that Pip's going to become a rich gentleman,' he said. 'But we're   30
the best of friends and I shall miss him terribly. Money won't make me happy ... ' Then he could say no more.

Mr Jaggers listened to Joe quietly. When Joe stopped talking, Mr Jaggers said to me: 'Well, Mr Pip. You're going to become a gentleman. And the sooner you come to London, the better. Come in exactly one week's time. You can take a coach and come straight to me.' And he left us.

5   I thought of something and ran after Mr Jaggers.

'Mr Jaggers,' I said. 'I've some friends in town that I'd like to say goodbye to. Will the person who's giving me my great expectations allow this?'

'You may do as you please,' he said.

10   I ran home again. I found Joe sitting quietly by the kitchen fire. I sat down beside him. We did not say anything for a long time.

Biddy was sitting near us, sewing.

At last, I asked: 'Joe, have you told Biddy?'

15   'No,' replied Joe. 'You tell her, Pip.'

'I wish you would tell her, Joe,' I said.

'Pip's going to be a rich gentleman,' said Joe. 'I wish him happiness.'

Biddy stopped sewing. She said she was glad, but
20   she looked very worried.

I told them what Mr Jaggers had said. No one must ask any questions about my fortune. No one must know anything. All that could be said was that I had great expectations. And I was getting them from an unknown
25   person.

Biddy looked into the fire. She promised not to ask any questions. Joe made the same promise.

IN LONDON WITH HERBERT

Leaving home

On Monday, I went to town to buy some new clothes.
After that I went to Uncle Pumblechook's house. I was
very surprised by his behaviour. He suddenly behaved
as if we were good friends. He had never seemed to   5
like me before. This change was clearly because of my
great expectations.

On Friday morning I went to Miss Havisham's house.
I found her in the room with the long table, walking
around with her stick.   10

'Miss Havisham,' I said, 'since I last saw you, I've met
with great expectations. I'm very grateful.'

'Yes, yes,' she said. 'I've seen Mr Jaggers. I've heard
all about it, Pip. So you're going to London tomorrow?'

'Yes, Miss Havisham.'

'And this fortune comes to you
from a very rich person?'

'Yes, Miss Havisham.'

'You don't know who it is?'

'No, Miss Havisham.'

'Well,' she said, 'be good, and
always do what Mr Jaggers
tells you. Goodbye, Pip.'

She held out her hand. I
went down on my knees
and kissed it. At that
time, I thought it
was the right
thing to do.

I would leave the village at five o'clock the next morning. I told Joe I wished to walk to the coach stop alone. I told myself that I was now a young gentleman, and did not need anyone to help me. But the truth was I did not want Joe to walk with me because I thought a gentleman should not be seen with a blacksmith. I was very ashamed of myself, but I still did not ask Joe to come.

The next morning, breakfast had no taste for me and I ate it quickly.

'Well, I suppose I must be off!' I said.

I said goodbye to my sister and Biddy. When it came to Joe's turn, I threw my arms around his neck. I almost cried. Then I took up my bag and walked out.

They stood at the door after I had gone. Biddy put her hands to her face. She was crying.

I walked on quickly. I was happy to be going to London. I had thought I would not be sad to leave home. But a moment later I burst into tears. I reached the sign-post at the end of the village. I put my hand on it and said:

'Goodbye, my dear, dear friend!'

Herbert Pocket

When I reached London, Mr Jaggers' clerk, Wemmick, took me to Herbert Pocket's rooms. Herbert Pocket was the son of my teacher, Mr Matthew Pocket.

Wemmick led me to a very old street. Then we went up some dirty, dusty stairs. Herbert's rooms were at the top of the stairs. There was a piece of paper stuck on the door, saying, 'I shall be back in a short while.'

I waited half an hour. At last Herbert came. He must have run all the way home because he was out of breath.

'Dear Mr Pip,' he said, 'I'm so sorry to be late. My father thought you would like to spend the day with me. I'll show you around London. I'm sorry that these rooms aren't very good. I'm not rich, you see, and neither is my father, so I have to work for a living. This is your bedroom, and that one is mine. I hope we shan't fight!'

As I stood listening to him, I knew I had met him before.

'You,' I said, 'are the pale young gentleman who fought me at Miss Havisham's house!'

We stared at each other.

'Of course! How strange that we should meet again!' cried Herbert. 'I hope you will forgive me for knocking you down?'

It was I who knocked him down! He had lost the fight badly. But I did not remind him.

'You were unlucky when I knocked you down,' Herbert continued, 'but you are very lucky now! You're going to inherit a fortune, I hear. You know, when we fought, I was hoping to get some money too. Miss Havisham asked me to visit her to see if she liked me. But she didn't. If she had, I might have married Estella.'

'Were you unhappy because she didn't like you?' I asked him.

'Oh, I didn't care much about it. Estella is a very difficult person to please. Very proud! Miss Havisham has looked after Estella since she was a child. She has taught her to hate all men.'

'But why?' I asked, surprised.

'Oh, Mr Pip! Don't you know?'

'No.'

'Dear me! It's quite a long story.'

I begged Herbert to tell me.

Miss Havisham's story

'Miss Havisham's mother died when she was a baby.
Her father was a very rich man and he always gave
her everything she wanted. They were very proud,
both the father and the daughter. But her father had
another son, not by his wife. This was kept a secret,
and Miss Havisham did not know anything about her
brother.

'Then the boy's mother died, and Miss Havisham was
told about her brother. He came to live in the house.
When the father died, he left his money to both his
children. But Miss Havisham's share was very much
more than her brother's. Well, her brother was weak
and foolish. He wasted his money, and when he had
none left, he borrowed some more.

'Then Miss Havisham fell in love with a man. He
pretended to love her too, but he was only interested
in her money. She gave him whatever he asked for —
and he asked for a lot.

'My father, Matthew Pocket, is Miss Havisham's
cousin, and he told her the truth — that this man didn't
really love her; he only wanted her money. But
Miss Havisham wouldn't listen. She loved the man too
much. She ordered my father to leave her house. Since
that day, my father and Miss Havisham haven't seen
each other.

'Some time later, the man agreed to marry
Miss Havisham. The wedding day was fixed, the
wedding dress was made, and the guests were invited.
On the morning of the wedding, the man sent
Miss Havisham a letter. It said that he no longer wanted
to marry her. He was never seen again.'

'But why didn't he marry her and get all her money?'
I asked.

'He was already married to someone else.
I heard that he got into a lot of trouble soon
afterwards, but I don't know where he is now.'

Joe brings some news

On Monday morning, Herbert went to the office of the
shipping company, where he worked. In the afternoon,
we went to Hammersmith, about six miles west of
London. Herbert told me that I would live there with
Mr Matthew Pocket and his family.

After two or three days, Mr Matthew Pocket and I
had a long talk. He told me how I must live. Mr Jaggers
had said that I should not become a businessman. I was
not to do any kind of work at all. All I had to do was
to learn to be a gentleman. This meant that I had to
become well-educated. I began to study very hard.

I decided to take one of Herbert's rooms in London.
I could stay there when I wanted a rest. In that way, I
would not become tired of studying. Also I knew
Herbert would like me to stay with him.

Mr Jaggers agreed to my plan.

One Monday morning, some months later, I received a letter from Biddy. It said that Joe was coming to London with Mr Wopsle. He would come to Herbert's rooms at nine o'clock on Tuesday morning.

I am sorry to say that I was not pleased to hear this. I was afraid my new friends would see Joe, and that they would laugh at him. Joe did not know how to behave with gentlemen.

On Tuesday morning Joe knocked at the door and I opened it.

'Pip, how are you, sir?'

'I am glad to see you, Joe.'

'How you have grown, sir!'

'And you, Joe, you look very healthy!'

'Yes, and your sister is in good health too, sir. And Biddy, she's well also, sir.'

'Joe,' I stopped him, 'how can you call me "sir"?'

Joe gave me a strange look. It was clear he felt that now I was a gentlemen, we could not be as friendly with each other as in the old days. He did not say anything, but his face showed how he felt. He was not at ease with me.

Herbert and I then had breakfast with Joe. After Herbert had gone to his office, Joe said:

'Now that we're alone, Pip, I must tell you something. It's about Miss Havisham. I was at the inn in our village one night, and Pumblechook came up to me and said: "Joseph, Miss Havisham wants to speak to you."

'Next day,' Joe continued, 'I put on my best clothes and went to see her. She said to me: "Mr Gargery, Pip writes to you, doesn't he?"

'I had received a letter from you, so I said, "Yes". Then she said: "Would you tell Pip that Estella has come home? She would be glad to see him."

'When I went home, Biddy said: "I am sure Pip would like to hear this news from you. So you go up to London and see him."

'Well, I've finished what I wanted to say, sir. And I wish you a long life and good health.' Joe stood up. 5

'But you're not going already, Joe?'

'Yes, I am. Pip, dear boy, I feel uncomfortable when I'm not at the old forge. If you wish to see me, Pip, just come and put your head in at the forge window. Then you'll see Joe the blacksmith at work. Goodbye, dear Pip.'

I went back to our town the next day. I knew I ought to stay in the village, with Joe. But I began to find excuses for not staying with him. I said to myself that I did not want to trouble him. He would not be expecting me to come. He would not have a bed ready for me. The truth was that I did not want to stay at my old home. I was a gentleman now, and I felt 20 uncomfortable with Joe. I decided to stay at the hotel.

A VERY UNEXPECTED VISITOR

Changes

I woke up early the next morning. It was too early to go to Miss Havisham's house, so I went for a walk. I thought about my expectations and all that
5 Miss Havisham had done for me. The more I thought about it, the more I was sure that she must have planned for Estella and me to be married one day. Then we would live together in her house when she died.

When I rang the bell at Miss Havisham's house, I got
10 a surprise. The gate was opened by Old Orlick. He was Miss Havisham's servant now, he told me. He was just as unpleasant as ever.

'Shall I go up to see Miss Havisham?' I asked.

'You know your way,' growled Orlick.

15 I found Miss Havisham sitting at the table. She was wearing the same dress. I knew now that it was her wedding dress from long ago. Near her was a beautiful young lady. She lifted up her eyes and looked at me. It was Estella. I did not know what to say.

20 'Do you find Estella much changed, Pip?' asked Miss Havisham.

'When I came in, Miss Havisham, I didn't know her at all. Now, she seems just like the old ...'

'What? Are you going to say the old Estella?'
25 Miss Havisham asked. 'She was proud and unkind. Don't you remember?'

I said that was a long time ago. Estella smiled, and said that I was quite right. In those days, she said, she had not been a kind person.

'Is he changed?' Miss Havisham asked Estella. 'Does he look like a gentleman now?'

Estella did not say anything. She just laughed quietly.

The three of us talked together for a little while. Then Miss Havisham sent us to walk in the garden.

Estella and I went into the garden. It was the same garden where I had had the fight with the pale young gentleman.

'Herbert and I are great friends now,' I told Estella.

'You must have changed your friends since you became a gentleman,' she said. 'Your old friends can hardly be your friends now.'

When she said this, I decided not to go and see Joe during my stay.

A visit from Mr Jaggers

We returned to the house. Estella told me that Jaggers had come from London to see Miss Havisham. He would be taking dinner with us. I began to push Miss Havisham around the room in her wheelchair. She was very weak now, and could not walk well.

Suddenly, Mr Jaggers came into the room. I felt Miss Havisham tremble. I noticed that she was afraid of him.

Mr Jaggers came up to us and said: 'Shall I push your chair, Miss Havisham? Why are you here, Pip?'

'Miss Havisham asked me to come and see Estella,' I replied.

5   When he heard this, he stared hard at me. I felt as if he could see what was in my heart.

'How often have you seen Estella before?' he asked. 'Twice? In any case, you can't have seen her for a long time. Why, you hardly know her!'

10   'Jaggers!' said Miss Havisham. 'Stop worrying, Pip. Go with him to have your dinner.'

After dinner, I agreed to meet Estella when she came to London. Then we said goodbye, and Mr Jaggers and I went to the hotel.

15   I did not sleep much that night. I kept thinking of Estella. I forgot all about Joe.

Next morning, I told Mr Jaggers what I knew about Orlick. I did not think he should be working for Miss Havisham.

20   'Yes, it's an old story,' said Mr Jaggers when I had finished. 'Miss Havisham can't tell who are good men and who are bad. I'll go to the house later on and send Orlick away. When I have talked to him, he won't make any trouble about leaving. He'll be afraid to.'

25   ## Estella comes to London

I was back in London that evening. After dinner with Herbert, I finally told him that I was in love with Estella.

'But she seems a thousand miles away from me,' I said. 'My future's so uncertain. I've no money of my 30 own and I depend on one person for everything. What if that person changes her — or his — mind? And what exactly are my expectations? In short, dear Herbert — should I hope for Estella?'

Herbert listened very carefully. He told me that in his opinion I should keep hoping. He went on to say that he too was in love.

'Her name is Clara,' he said, 'and she lives in London, by the river. Her father worked on a ship, but now he's sick and can't work any more. He lies in bed all day, watching the boats on the river.'

Herbert went on to say that he wanted to marry Clara, but he could only do so when he started to earn money. She was not at all rich, and neither was he.

One day, a letter came for me from Estella. This was all it said:

> *I am coming to London the day after tomorrow on the midday coach. Miss Havisham says that you have agreed to meet me. Therefore, I am writing this letter to remind you.*
>
> *Yours, Estella.*

I was very excited. I could hardly wait until I saw Estella's face again. At last the day arrived, and I was helping Estella to get down from the coach. She was more beautiful than ever.

'I'm going to Richmond,' she said. 'You'll have to take me, as I don't know the way. We have to do what we're told, you and I.'

She told me that she was going to live with a lady in Richmond, which is nine miles to the west of London. The lady would take her to parties and dances. In this way, Estella would meet a lot of rich young gentlemen.

The funeral

One evening, I was sitting at home when a letter arrived. It brought sad news. My sister had died one or two days ago. She would be buried the following Monday.

My sister had been unkind to me when I was a boy, but I was sorry to hear of her death. I wrote to Joe to say how sorry I was. On Monday, I took the earliest coach to our town and walked to Joe's forge.

After the funeral, Biddy, Joe and I had dinner together. It was not a happy meal and I felt very uncomfortable. We ate in the best room in the house. In the past, we had always eaten in the kitchen. I felt that Joe and Biddy were acting as if we were strangers because I was now a gentleman.

After dinner, Joe and I went out to the forge. We sat down together on the large stone outside. Joe smoked his pipe. It was almost like the old days when I was his apprentice. I told Joe I wanted to sleep in my own little room. This pleased him very much.

In the evening, I went with Biddy for a walk in the garden. Biddy talked about Joe and how much he loved me.

'Biddy,' I said, 'I have decided that from now on, I shall come back more often. I am not going to leave poor Joe alone.'

She did not say anything, but I could see that she did not believe me. I was not pleased with this. Biddy did not think I would come to see Joe. I did not know why she should think so. I felt so angry that I hardly spoke to Biddy again for the rest of my visit.

Early in the morning, I went back to London. Before I went, I looked in through the window of the forge.

'Goodbye, Joe! I'll come back soon, and often.'

'That would make me very happy,' said Joe. 'I am glad, dear Pip.'

But Biddy was quite right. I did not go back again for a long time.

An old friend

One night, just after my twenty-third birthday, I was sitting reading in my London rooms. I was alone, as Herbert had gone away on business for a few days. I had recently used some of my money to help him. I wanted my dear friend to share my good fortune. But I had not told him anything about it, and he did not know what I had done for him.

The evening was rainy and windy, and I was lonely without Herbert. Suddenly I heard footsteps on the stairs. I took my lamp and went and stood at the top of the stairs. All was quiet.

'Is someone down there?' I called out.

'Yes,' said a voice, but I could see nothing in the darkness.

'Which floor do you want to go to?'

'To the top floor — I have come to see Mr Pip.'

'That's my name. Is anything wrong?'

'Nothing is wrong,' replied the voice. And a man came up.

He was dressed in warm, thick clothes. His hair was long and grey. His skin was brown, as if he had been at sea for a long time. He was about sixty years of age, but he looked very strong. He came to the top of the stairs. Then he did a very strange thing. He held out both his hands to me as if I was an old friend. I was very surprised.

'What do you want?' I asked him.

'What do I want?' he replied. 'Ah, yes! I'll tell you.'

'Do you wish to come in?' I asked him.

'Yes,' he replied. 'I wish to come in, master.'

I did not know why he called me 'master', and I was not pleased that he wanted to come in. But I took him into the room.

He looked around him carefully. Then he held out his hands to me once again.

'What do you mean?' I asked. I thought he was mad.

'I've wanted to meet you for a long time,' he replied. 'And I've come from far away to do it. Oh, I'm so happy to see you!'

Then he looked around the room again and asked, 'Is no one else here?'

'Who are you? Why do you come to my rooms at this time of the night and ask me that question?' I said sharply.

'You're a brave one,' he replied. 'I'm glad that you have grown up to be brave.'

Suddenly I knew him. He was my prisoner!

I begin to understand

He held out both his hands again. I did not know what
to do, so I put my hands into his. He held them tightly.
Then he kissed them. He would not let go.

'You were very kind to me, dear Pip,' he said. 'I have   5
never forgotten your kindness.'

He wanted to hold me in his arms. But I held him
back.

'Don't do that!' I said. 'I'm glad you are pleased
about what I did. But you didn't have to come here to   10
thank me. I will not ask you to go. But you must
understand ...'

'What?' he asked. 'What must I understand?'

'Things are different now,' I replied. 'I can't see you
again. I'm glad that you've come to thank me. But we   15
can't stay together. You must go your way. I must go
mine ...' I stopped, seeing that his eyes were full of
tears.

When I saw his tears, I felt sorry for him. I could not
turn him out of my rooms. I poured drinks for both of   20
us, and sat down near him.

'I'm sorry,' I said. 'I don't mean to be rude. Please
forget what I said just now. I wish you health and
happiness.'

He put out his hand. I gave him mine. Then I asked   25
him: 'How are you living now?'

'I've been a farmer in Australia, thousands of miles
away,' he replied, 'and I've done very well, dear boy.
In fact, I am rich! You know, many prisoners are sent
to Australia, to stay there till they die. Many become   30
rich. But I'm the richest of them all!'

'I'm glad to hear it.'

'And you, Pip? You must have had good luck too, I
think. Here you are in these nice rooms! The last time

I saw you, you lived with a blacksmith. What's happened since then?'

I told him about my great expectations, and that I was going to inherit a fortune.

'May I ask whose fortune?' he said.

'I do not know.'

'Let me guess how much money you get each year,' he said. 'The first number — is it five?'

He was right! I jumped up from my chair. I stared at him, trembling with fear.

'Now, there must be someone who looks after your money until you are older, too. Your man is a lawyer, is he not? The first letter of his name — is it J?'

In a flash I understood everything.

It was not Miss Havisham who had been giving me money. She did not have any plans about Estella and me. She had not wanted Estella to marry me. Estella would never be mine. The money which made me a gentleman had come from a prisoner!

Provis Tells His Story

A second father

The more I looked at the man sitting in front of me,
the worse I felt about myself. It was because of this
bad, old man, that I have left dear Joe and Biddy. It
was because of him that I had treated them so badly.   5

While I was thinking about this, he went on talking.

'Yes, my dear Pip, I have made you a gentleman.
Whatever money I have will be yours one day. You
once gave food to a poor prisoner, dear boy. That
prisoner became successful. He was so successful that   10
he could make someone a gentleman. You're that
gentleman, Pip.'

I could not breathe. I thought I would faint. And still
the man continued.

'Do you see, Pip? I'm your second father. You're my   15
son. Why, I love you more than a son. I've saved my
money and it's all for you to spend. When I was sent
to Australia, I looked after sheep, and when I was with
them, I would go for months without seeing a human
face. But I saw yours, Pip. I kept seeing your face. I   20
said to myself: "If ever I become rich, I'll make that boy
a gentleman." And I have done it! Dear boy! You are
my gentleman!'

Again he took both my hands, and kissed them.

'Don't try to talk,' he said. 'You must keep quiet, dear   25
boy. I have wanted to meet you for so long. Did you
ever think that it was me who sent you your fortune?'

'Oh no, no!' I whispered.

'Well, you see, it was me, and only me. No one
knows about this, except Mr Jaggers and me.   30

'It wasn't easy for me to leave Australia. It wasn't safe, either. I was sent there for the rest of my life. If the police find out that I have come back, I will be hanged. But I did it, dear boy, I did it! Now, where shall I stay?' he asked. 'I must have a place to sleep, my boy.'

'My friend is away — you can sleep in his room.'

'Dear boy, we must be very careful. Nobody else must know about me.'

I locked the door with trembling hands. Then I showed him Herbert's room and he went to bed. I sat by the fire, trying to think about what had happened.

The happiness of Abel Magwitch

I could not hide him in my rooms. There was a woman who came to clean the place. She would talk about him to other people. I would have to tell her that he was an uncle of mine. The next morning, his door opened and he came out. I was not happy to see him.

'I don't even know your name,' I said.

He said that he had taken the name of Provis.

'What's your real name?' I asked.

'Abel Magwitch,' he replied. He sat down, looking at me. 'So this is the gentleman I have made! How happy I am, Pip! All I want to do is to sit and look at you.'

Then he took a thick wallet from his pocket and put it on the table. It was full of money.

'This money is for you, dear boy. Don't be afraid to take it. I've come to England for one purpose. I want to see my gentleman spend his money. He must spend it like a gentleman. That's all I want — to see you spend money like a gentleman.' 5

'Stop!' I cried. 'How am I going to keep you safe? How long are you going to stay here? What plans do you have?'

'Well, dear boy, the danger isn't very great. If nobody tells the police about me, there's nothing to fear. Jaggers 10 knows about me. So does his clerk, and so do you. Nobody else knows. So who is there to tell the police? No, I'm not going back to Australia. I've come to live in England until I die.'

'Where are you going to live? Where will you be safe?' 15

'Dear boy, I don't know where I'll live or how I'll live. Tell me what you think.'

I decided to find Provis a room in a house nearby. This seemed the safest thing to do. Herbert would come back in two or three days' time. One thing was clear 20 to me. I would have to tell Herbert about Provis.

I knew of a quiet house not far from ours and I was able to get a room there for Provis. After I got the room, I went to see Mr Jaggers.

When he saw me, he stood up slowly. I could see 25 that he already knew what I had come to tell him.

'Don't say any name to me,' he said. 'You understand, no name. Don't tell me anything.'

In this way, Mr Jaggers could honestly say: 'Nobody told me that Provis had come back to England.' This 30 was important as Mr Jaggers was a lawyer. If somebody told him about Provis, he would have to report it to the police. Whether he knew or not was another matter.

'Mr Jaggers, I want to make certain that what he told me is true.' 35

'It's quite true,' he replied.

'But I always thought that my expectations would come from Miss Havisham.'

'I never told you that,' said Mr Jaggers.

My last hopes were ended. I had nothing more to ask. I left Mr Jaggers and went back to Provis.

Provis must leave England

One evening after dinner, I heard footsteps on the stairs. I knew it was Herbert. Provis jumped up from his chair with a knife in his hand.

'It's all right! It's Herbert,' I said. Herbert came in.

'Pip, my dear friend, how are you?' he said. 'You look so thin and pale! Have you been ill?'

Then he saw that someone else was in the room.

'Oh, I beg your pardon!' he said.

Provis put away his knife. I closed the door and said to Herbert, 'Something very strange has happened. This is … a visitor who has come to see me.'

'It's all right, dear boy,' said Provis. 'You can tell him about me. But he must promise not to tell anyone else.'

Herbert promised. Then all three of us sat in front of the fire. I told Herbert all that Provis had told me. He became as worried as I was. At midnight Provis left for his rooms. Herbert and I were glad to see him go.

We tried to think what we should do. I told Herbert I would not take any more money from Provis.

'But I've already taken so much money,' I continued, 'and I've spent it all. Why, I even owe money to people. What can I pay them with? How can I earn money? All I know is how to be a gentleman. I'm fit for nothing else.'

'You mustn't say that,' said Herbert. 'You know, recently I've been very lucky at my work. Perhaps you

could come to work with me. But first we must get
Provis out of England. You must go too. He'll go
anywhere with you. And we must find out why Provis
was sent to prison.'

Provis tells his story

Next morning after breakfast, I said to Provis: 'It's
strange that I know so little about you after all you have
done for me.'

'Well,' he said, 'I could tell you my story in a few
words. I have been in prison, out of prison, in prison
and out of prison. I have been punished in all kinds of
ways except hanging. I have been taken here and I
have been taken there. I have been sent out of one
town after another. I do not know where I was born.
When I was a child, I had to steal food to eat. I moved
from place to place. I begged and I stole. I worked
where I could get work. In this way, I grew up to be
a man.

'Then, more than twenty years ago, I met a man
called Compeyson. I was fighting with him when you
and the soldiers found us on the marshes, Pip. If I see
him again, I'll kill him.

'Compeyson was looking for somebody to work for
him, to go stealing with him. I was very poor, so I
agreed to do his work. But he was clever. He was never
caught. I was always the one in trouble. And he never
gave me enough money. I had to borrow from him. I
owed him money all the time. I could not stop working
for him. If I stopped, I would have to pay him his
money back.

'Compeyson was younger than me. But he made me
do everything he wanted.

'At last, we were both caught. He blamed me. The
police believed him — who wouldn't? He was educated

and looked like a gentleman, and he'd never been in trouble before. But I'm rough and common, and the police knew my face well. So I was given a heavier punishment. He was sent to the prison-ship for seven years. But I was sent there for fourteen.'

Miss Havisham's lover

'I decided to kill Compeyson, but for a very long time,
10 I could not get near him. Then one day I saw my chance. I came up behind him and cut his face. Somebody saw me, and I was stopped. I was put in the bottom of the ship, but I escaped and swam to the shore. I was hiding in the churchyard when I first saw
15 you, Pip. I learnt from you, my boy, that Compeyson had also escaped. He was hiding in the marshes. He must have escaped because he wanted to get away from me. He didn't know that I had escaped before him.

'I searched through the marshes for him and I caught
20 him. I wanted to do the worst thing I could to him, so I gave him to the soldiers. I did not care what happened to me. I wanted Compeyson to be punished.

'But his punishment was less than mine. As usual, everybody thought I was the worse man. I was sent to
25 live in Australia for the rest of my life. But I didn't stay there. And so, dear sirs, here I am.'

'Is Compeyson dead?' I asked.

'I don't know,' Provis replied. 'But if he's alive, I'm sure he hates me greatly.'

Herbert had been writing in a book. He pushed the book towards me. Provis did not see us. He was looking at the fire. Herbert had written:

Compeyson was the man who pretended to love Miss Havisham.

I shut the book. Herbert saw that I understood his note. We both looked at Provis. His story made me even more worried. I was afraid that Compeyson might still be alive. What would happen if he found out that Provis had returned to England?

Very bad news

Provis left us in the evening. After talking about what he had told us, Herbert and I decided to take him to France. However, we did not tell Provis about this straight away. We needed time to think.

I told Herbert that I wanted to see Miss Havisham and Estella before I left England. We decided to tell Provis about our plans after my return.

First I went to Richmond, but I was told that Estella had gone to Miss Havisham. The next day, I told Provis that I was going to see Joe. Poor Joe! Until then I had almost forgotten him. I would be away for one night. I went by the early morning coach, and reached the town hotel before breakfast time. At the hotel, I was surprised to see one of Mr Pocket's pupils. His name was Drummle, and he was a gentleman. He was also a cruel and violent man. I and the other pupils disliked Drummle very much.

I did not want to speak to Drummle, and he did not want to speak to me. We pretended not to see each other. This went on for some time. Then accidentally his eyes met mine. However, he still did not speak to me. Instead, he spoke to the waiter who had brought my breakfast.

'Waiter,' he said loudly, 'bring my horse to the door. But not the lady's horse; she won't be riding today. And I won't have my dinner here this evening; I'll be eating at the lady's house. Do you understand?'

It was clear that Drummle wanted me to hear what he was saying. But I did not know which lady he meant. Then he went out.

After breakfast, I went to Miss Havisham's house. I found both Estella and Miss Havisham there. They told me a piece of very bad news. It was the worst news I could ever have heard.

Estella was the lady that Drummle had spoken about. She had met him at Richmond. She was going to marry him.

Miss Havisham looked at my face. She saw that my heart was broken, just as her own heart had been broken. When she saw this, she gave a long, low cry. Then she took my hand and held it tightly.

'I was wrong!' she whispered. 'Can you forgive me, Pip? I know the pain that I have made you feel. Forgive me! Tell me, is there anything I can do for you, Pip? You must let me help you!'

I told her to help Herbert instead. I had wanted to buy him a share in his shipping business. This would make him one of the owners. But I was not able to do this now. Miss Havisham agreed to do what I asked her.

I thanked her, and left. I could not bear to stay any longer.

PROVIS GOES INTO HIDING

Herbert's plan

It was past midnight when I reached London. I walked quickly towards our rooms. Herbert had expected me to be back in the morning, but I had my own key. I could get in without waking him.   5

The watchman of the place looked at me very carefully. I told him my name.

'Yes, I thought it was you, sir,' said the watchman, 'but I wasn't sure. This note was brought for you.'

I took the note. On its cover was written: *Please read*   10
this here. I opened it. It was from Mr Jaggers' clerk, Wemmick. It said: *Do not go home*.

As soon as I read this, I walked away. I stayed the night in a hotel.

The next morning I got up early to meet Wemmick   15
on his way to Mr Jaggers' office.

'Hallo, Pip,' he said, when he saw me, 'you're back then!'

'Yes,' I replied, 'but I haven't been home yet.'

'I'm very glad of that,' he said. Then he told me why   20
he had left the note for me. He did not mention the name Provis (for the same reason as Mr Jaggers), but I knew who he was talking about. He said some people had found out that Provis had left Australia. They were looking for him. They had guessed that he would come   25
to me. And they had been watching my rooms.

'Who are they?' I asked.

'I'm afraid to say who they are,' he replied.

'Have you heard of a man named Compeyson? Is he here in London?' I asked.   30

Wemmick would not answer, but he nodded his head twice. Then he said: 'When I heard that somebody had returned from Australia, I went to your rooms. But you weren't there, so I went to Mr Herbert's office. I asked
5   whether anybody was in or near your rooms. I told him to hide that person somewhere while you were away.

'Mr Herbert thought of a plan. He told me that there was a room in Miss Clara's house. The person could stay there for a while.

10   'I thought this was a very good plan, for three reasons. Firstly, Miss Clara's house is far away from your rooms. No one will look for him there. Secondly, you don't have to go there. Mr Herbert often goes to Miss Clara's house. He'll tell you any news about the
15   person. Thirdly, the house is near the river. It'll be easy to get him to a ship when it's safe.'

This plan made me feel much happier. I thanked Wemmick and asked him to tell me more.

'Well, sir,' he said, 'Mr Herbert got the person into
20   Miss Clara's house safely. We've done everything we can now. You can see the person tonight, before you go back to your rooms. If you stay away from your rooms until night-time, there should be no danger.'

The rowers

25   At eight o'clock in the evening, I went to Miss Clara's house. I found Provis in a room at the top of the house. The windows of the room faced the river. He did not seem to be worried. Herbert and I sat with him by the fire. I told him about what Wemmick had said about
30   somebody watching my rooms.

'We must stay away from each other for some time,' I said gently. 'I'm afraid that the people watching my rooms might follow me here. And you must leave

England soon. I'll come with you if it's safe. If not, I'll come to you later.'

Provis said he would do what Wemmick said. Wemmick would know what was the best thing to be done.   5

Herbert then had another idea.

'We can both row a boat well, Pip,' he said. 'Why don't you and I take Provis down the river ourselves? We could have a boat ready on the river. If we row up and down the river a few times, people will get used   10
to seeing us. They won't take any notice of us after a while.'

Provis and I thought this was a good idea.

Herbert and I got ready to leave, and I said goodbye to Provis. I would not see him again until we left England.   15

The next day, I got a boat and began to go out rowing. Sometimes I went alone, and sometimes with Herbert. After a few times, nobody took much notice of us.

Nothing happened for a few weeks. We heard nothing from Wemmick. Meanwhile, I was becoming very worried about money. I had given the wallet back to Provis, but I had little money of my own. I had to borrow more and more,   25
and I did not know how I could ever pay it all back.

I worried even more about Compeyson. What would happen if he found out about Provis?

And so the days passed. I rowed up and down the river, and I waited for a message from Wemmick.

At last, a message came from Wemmick. It said:

> *Burn this paper after you have read it. You may do what you want to do early this week. If you want to try, you can do it on Wednesday.*

I showed the message to Herbert. Then I burnt it in the fire. We planned what we should do.

'I have thought very hard about this,' said Herbert. 'I think we should take Startop to help us.' Startop was another of Mr Pocket's pupils, and I liked him very much. 'He is a good friend, and a good boatman. I'm sure he'll help us. We won't tell him everything — just that we must get Provis on to a ship out of England for a very important reason. Will you go away with Provis, Pip?'

'Yes,' I replied.

I did not care where Provis and I went. The important thing was to get him out of England. First, we would row him along the river towards the sea. Then we would stop any steamship which passed by. We would go on the first steamship that would take us.

We planned to get down the river a day earlier. We would then wait in the boat at some quiet place. When a steamship passed by, we would stop it.

Herbert would go to see Provis that night, to tell him the plan. On Wednesday morning, we would row down to Miss Clara's house. When he saw us from his window, Provis was to come down and get into the boat quickly. After this had been arranged, Herbert went to his office.

The old building on the marshes

An hour later, another letter arrived. It was very dirty, but quite well written. It said:

> *If you are not afraid, come to the marshes near*
> *your old village. Come tonight or tomorrow night*   5
> *at nine o'clock. Come to the old building. You will*
> *find out something about your Uncle Provis. Tell*
> *no one and come alone.*

I already had so many things to think about. I could not decide what to do about this letter, and I had to   10
make up my mind quickly. If I wanted to go to the marshes, I had to take the afternoon coach. I could not wait until the next day, Tuesday, and go that night. What if I did not return in time for our plan on Wednesday morning? I decided to go that afternoon. I   15
did not know what that person would tell me. But it might mean we had to change our plan.

The letter had said that I must tell no one. So I left a note for Herbert saying that I was going to see Miss Havisham before I left England. It was dark before   20
the coach reached the town. I had dinner in the hotel, and waited until it was time to go to the old building.

It was a dark, cold night. My long walk to the old building was lonely. There seemed to be no one but myself outside on the marshes. At last I arrived. There   25
was a candle burning at a window, but no one seemed to be inside. I pushed open the door, and went in.

'Is anyone here?' I called out.

No one answered. I looked at my watch. It was past nine. I called out again but there was still no answer.   30

I knew that there must be someone else in the hut. Someone must have lit the candle. I decided to look around carefully. I turned to pick up the candle so that I could see better.

Suddenly it went out.

Then a rope was thrown over my head. My hands
⁵ were pulled tightly to my sides.

'Now,' a voice growled, 'I've got you!'

'What's this?' I cried. 'Who is it?'

I could see nothing — it was too dark.

A strong hand was put over my mouth to stop me
¹⁰ from calling out. It was a man's hand. In a moment I was tied to the wall.

Then the man lit the candle. I felt cold inside when I saw his face. It was Orlick!

'Now I've got you!' he cried again.

'Let me go!'

'Ah!' he said, 'I'll let you go … afterwards. Oh, you enemy, you enemy!'

He sat looking at me. Then he reached down and picked up a gun.

'You had me sent away from Miss Havisham's, you did.'

'What else could I do?' I said.

'You did more than that. You came between me and a young woman I liked. My Biddy! You made her hate Old Orlick.'

'You killed your own sister!'

'No,' I said, 'you yourself made her hate you.'

'You wanted to send me out of this country. You did all you could, didn't you? Too bad you didn't get rid of me, dog. Too bad. Because now I'm going to get rid of you. Ever since you were a child, you've been cruel to me. Always in Old Orlick's way. Tonight, you'll get out of his way. I'll have no more of you!'

He drank brandy from a bottle now and then while he talked. The more he drank, the angrier he became. I knew that when the brandy was finished, Orlick would put an end to me.

'Animal!' he shouted. 'You killed your own sister, you know. Yes, you are to blame! I came upon her from behind. I struck her down. But you are to blame, not Old Orlick. You got your holiday but I got a beating. You killed your sister. And tonight, you'll pay for it!'

He took another drink. Then he stood looking at me silently. At last, he said:

'I've wanted to kill you, ever since you were here for your sister's funeral. I have followed you wherever you went. And now I have found your Uncle Provis.

'Old Orlick shall get rid of you tonight. There are others who'll get rid of your Uncle Provis. He has been watched too. I know your Uncle Provis's real name. Let Magwitch watch out for Compeyson.'

He drank the last drop from the bottle. He bent down. I saw him pick up a stone hammer. It had a long, heavy handle. He came slowly towards me.

I shouted out as loudly as I could.

Then I heard voices calling to me. The door was pushed open. Some men rushed in and seized Orlick, but he got away from them. I saw him run away into the darkness. Then I fainted.

ON THE RIVER

Rescued

When I opened my eyes, I found that I was lying on the floor. My hands were untied. I heard somebody say: 'I think he's all right.'

5 I looked up, and saw Herbert looking down at me. Startop was with him. Then I thought of Provis. I tried to get up, but fell back again. There was a terrible pain in my arm.

'Is it too late, Herbert?' I asked. 'How long have I 10 been here?'

'Dear Pip,' said Herbert, 'it's still Monday night. You can rest the whole day tomorrow.'

Then he told me that I had accidentally dropped Orlick's letter in our rooms. Herbert and Startop found

it and they became worried. They came after me by coach. They could not find me at the hotel or at Miss Havisham's house. Then they found a boy who had seen the way I had gone.

He brought them to the old building on the marshes. They reached it just as I shouted for help. Thank God they heard me, and were there to rescue me.

All three of us went back to London by coach that night. It was daylight when we reached our rooms.   5

I went to bed at once and slept all day.

Rowing to freedom

Wednesday morning came. The sun was shining brightly, but it was cold and there was a strong wind. We put on our thick coats and set off to the place where   10 I kept my boat. I did not think about where I was going, or when I would come back to England. All I thought of was Provis's safety.

Herbert and Startop rowed. I was too weak to help them much. We planned to get to a wide and lonely   15 part of the river before dark. We would spend the night at an inn there.

There was a steamship going to Hamburg on Thursday morning. It would start from London at about nine. The steamship to Rotterdam would also start at   20 the same time. We knew they would both be passing near us. We would row out to meet the first one that passed by. If it would not take us, then we would try the second.

Very soon we reached Miss Clara's house. As soon   25 as Provis saw us, he came down to the river and got quickly into the boat. In a minute we were off again.

'Dear boy!' said Provis as he sat down. 'Thank you, thank you!'

Provis was not worried at all. He never thought of   30 danger. As long as danger was still far away, he never worried about it. He said that the time to worry was when the danger was close by.

'You do not know how happy I am, dear boy,' he said to me. 'All these years I have been in prison. Day by day, I had to sit between four walls. But now, I am free. I am happy to sit here quietly beside you. You do not know how happy I am!'

'I think I know what freedom means,' I said.

'Ah,' he said, 'but you have always been free. To know what freedom really is, you must have been a prisoner.'

'If nothing happens,' I said, 'you will be safe and free again in a few hours.'

'Well,' he replied, 'I hope so.'

We rowed all day. Little by little, the river grew wider. Soon it became dark.

We looked for an inn where we could stay for the night. At last, we saw one.

It was rather dirty, but there was a warm fire in the kitchen and good food to eat and drink. After a large supper, we went to bed.

Waiting for the steamships

We woke up early the next morning and went down to the boat. By midday we were waiting at the place where the steamships would pass by.

Half an hour later, we saw smoke. A steamship was coming. At that moment I saw another rowing boat coming from the shore. It was a little way in front of us. It was going in the same direction as us.

The steamship was now very close. It was the *Hamburg*. I called to Herbert and Startop to row out. In this way, the people on the steamship could see us waiting for them. Provis sat very still. He had wrapped himself up in his coat. His face could not be seen.

By now the other rowing boat had crossed in front of us. The men in it waited for us to come nearer. There were four men: two rowers, the man who was steering, and a fourth man. The fourth man seemed to be afraid of something. He too hid his face in his coat.   5

The *Hamburg* was coming towards us very fast. The noise of its engines grew louder and louder. It was almost on us. Then the man steering the other rowing boat called out to us.

'You have a prisoner with you. He has returned here   10
from Australia. His name is Abel Magwitch. He is also known as Provis. I ask him to give himself up.'

He steered his boat into ours. The rowers seized hold of the side of our boat. It happened so fast that we could do nothing. At the same time, the *Hamburg* kept   15
coming directly towards us. It was not starting to slow down. We were all in great danger. If the steamship hit us, we would surely drown.

I heard the people on the ship calling out to us. Someone shouted an order to stop the engines. But it   20
was too late.

Drowning

Our small boats began to rock violently in the rough water. The big waves made by the steamship were crashing all around us. Then Provis gave a shout and   25
jumped into the other boat. He pulled the coat away from the fourth man's face. I knew that face. It was Compeyson.

Compeyson tried to move away from Provis, but he slipped. With a cry of fear, he fell into the water. Waves   30
covered his head and he disappeared. Now the waves were so big that water came into our boat. It was filling up! We were sinking!

It all happened very
quickly. One minute I was
in the boat; the next I was
in the river. The waves were
5 too big — I couldn't swim.
Lights flashed inside my head
and I felt myself going down and down …
     Then I felt hands seize me and pull me up out of the
water. I saw I was in the other boat. Herbert and Startop
10 were there too. Our own boat was gone. I could not
see Provis or Compeyson.

The rowers were staring at the water for signs of Provis and Compeyson. Then I saw something dark coming towards us. It was Provis. He was lifted into the boat, and one of the men put chains on his legs.

The men continued to watch the water. The *Hamburg* sailed past us into the distance. The water became still again. But there was no sign of Compeyson. It was clear that he had drowned.

We were taken back to the inn where we had stayed the night before. Provis had been badly hurt in the chest, and he had a deep cut on his head. He had gone under the steamship when he fell into the water, and it had hit him. I was very worried about him.

We remained at the inn until the tide changed. Then Provis was placed in a police boat. He was to be taken back to London, and put on trial.

Herbert and Startop returned to London by coach. But I felt that I should go with Provis. I wanted to be with him for as long as he lived.

The good man

I did not hate him any more. I knew that he had wanted to be good to me. For many years, he had thought of only one thing. He wanted to repay the kindness that I did for him when I was a child. He was a good man, much better than I was. Provis had tried to repay my kindness to him, but I had never thought of repaying Joe's kindness to me. So I went with Provis in the boat. I told him how sorry I was. He had come to England because of me. And now he would be punished for it.

'Dear boy,' he said, 'I do not care what happens to me. I know my boy can become a gentleman without me. All my money will go to you.'

I knew that this was not so. By returning to England, Provis had broken the law. All his money would be taken by the government. There would be nothing for me. But I would never tell him this — not for all the money in the world. And I would make sure Jaggers and Wemmick did not tell him either. I wanted him to die happy.

'I will never leave you,' I said. 'You have been a great friend to me. I want to thank you.'

Tears came to his eyes. He turned away so that I could not see his face.

Herbert leaves London

It was not long after we had returned to London that Herbert had to leave me. He had to go to work in Cairo. Before he left, he told me that there was a clerk needed in the Cairo office.

'You know, Pip, I started working as a clerk. And look at me now — I'm one of the owners! What I'm trying to say is — in short, my dear friend, will you come to work with me in Cairo?'

'Dear Herbert, you're the best friend a man could have,' I replied. 'But just now I can't think of anything but Provis. Is it possible for you to wait a little before I give you my answer?'

'I'll wait as long as you like, Pip. Six months — a year ! But I'm afraid I must leave for Cairo on Saturday.'

A few days later, I said goodbye to him. He was full of hope and happiness. Clara would soon be joining him in Cairo as his wife. But he was sad to leave me.

Then I went back to my rooms. I felt very lonely. The rooms were no longer like a home to me. I felt that I had no home anywhere.

THE BEST OF FRIENDS

The death of Provis

All this time, Provis was very ill. He was in prison waiting for his trial. I visited him there every day.

His voice was weak and he spoke very little. But he was always ready to listen to me. I talked to him, and 5 read to him every day. I could see that he was slowly becoming weaker.

On the day of his trial, Provis was so weak he was allowed to sit down in court.

The trial was not a long one. It was a simple case. 10 Provis had been sent to live abroad for the rest of his life, but he had come back to England. He had broken the law, and the punishment for this was death. Therefore, Provis must die. He would be hanged.

I hoped and prayed that Provis would die because 15 of his illness. Then he would escape being hanged.

Soon afterwards, he became much worse. One morning I arrived at the prison and sat down at his bedside. He looked up at me with a strange look in his eyes. 20

'Dear boy,' he said, 'I thought you were late. But I knew you couldn't be late.'

'They have just opened the doors of the prison,' I said. 'I was waiting at the gate.'

'You always wait at the gate, don't you, dear boy?' 25

'Yes. I don't want to miss a moment with you.'

'Thank you, dear boy, thank you. You're always with me. You've never left me alone, dear boy.'

I pressed his hand gently. I could not forget that once I had wanted to leave him. 30

'One thing makes me very happy,' he said. 'You feel at ease with me now. Before, I know you felt uncomfortable with your rough prisoner. But you're fond of me now, I think. Yes, I'm very happy. I don't
5 mind having to die.'

He was breathing with great difficulty.

'Are you feeling any pain today?' I asked.

'Don't worry about it, dear boy,' he replied. 'I don't want to trouble you.'

'You never want to trouble me.'

But Provis did not reply. He lifted my hand to his lips. Then he held my hand in his.

Suddenly he let go. He was dead.

I am very ill

I was alone. Both Herbert and Provis had left me. It was at this terrible time that I became very ill. I lay in my bed, too ill to move. I did not know where I was.
20 My illness made me dream strange dreams. I dreamed that someone was taking care of me. I dreamed that I could see Joe's face. Dear Joe! He had always been so good to me.

After some time, I began to get better. But whenever
25 I opened my eyes, I saw Joe. Was I still dreaming? I could not see or think clearly. After some time I decided that there really was someone taking care of me. And one morning I felt strong enough to ask: 'Are you Joe?'

'Of course I am, dear Pip!' his kind voice answered.

He was really with me. I asked him if he had been there all the time.

'Almost all the time, dear boy. We received a letter about your illness. There was no one to take care of you. So I decided to visit you, and come and stay with you. You and I have always been the best of friends.'

The death of Miss Havisham

Time passed. Soon I could see and think more clearly. I did not feel so weak any more. When Joe saw that, he decided to tell me about Miss Havisham. She had died a week after I became ill. It was a terrible story. She had been sitting too near to a candle. Her long veil had begun to burn. It was so old, it burned as quickly as if it were paper. She could not be saved.

Joe also told me that Orlick was now in prison.

I was becoming stronger all the time. Joe took care of me. I felt as though I was a boy again.

As I became better, Joe became less at ease with me. He thought that I did not need him any more.

One morning, we were sitting by the river not far from my rooms. The sunlight was bright and warm. As we stood up to go home, I said:

'See, Joe! I can walk again quite strongly. Now you shall see me walk back by myself.'

'Don't try to do too much, Pip,' he said. 'But I am happy that you are able to walk now, sir.'

I felt hurt when he called me 'sir'. I knew what he was thinking, and I could not blame him for it. He thought that once I was well, I would begin to live like a gentleman again. And I had not been kind to him when I was a gentleman. I had been ashamed of him. I had never gone to see him. Why, I had almost forgotten about him. No, I could not blame him for thinking that I would become unfriendly again.

That night Joe came to my room when I was going to bed. He asked me whether I was feeling well.

5 'Yes, dear Joe, quite,' I replied.

Then he gently put his hand on my shoulder. In a low voice, he said: 'Good night!'

When I got up in the morning, he had gone. He had left me a letter. It said:

10 *I do not wish to stay too long. So I have gone. You are well again now, Pip. You do not need me any more. It's better for you that I go. We are always the best of friends.*

Joe and Biddy are married

As soon as I was well enough, I went to the forge. I had to see Joe. When I arrived, Joe and Biddy were standing outside.

At first Biddy was very surprised. Then she put her arms around me. I cried to see her, and she cried to see me. I cried because she looked so sweet and happy. She cried because I was so pale and thin.

'But, Biddy, you and Joe have your best clothes on!'

'It's my wedding day,' cried Biddy in great happiness. 'I've married Joe.'

I had not expected this at all. I was so surprised that I could not speak. After a minute or two, I said:

'Dear Biddy, you have the best husband in the whole world. And, dear Joe, you have the best wife in the whole world. May you both be very happy!

'And now,' I said, 'please tell me, both of you. Please tell me that you forgive me for being so unkind to you.' 5

'Oh, dear old Pip,' said Joe. 'God knows that I forgive you. But you've done nothing wrong. There's nothing for me to forgive.'

'And God knows that I forgive you too, Pip,' said Biddy gently. 10

I sold everything that belonged to me. I paid back the money which I owed. Then I went to work with Herbert in Cairo. Our company did very well. After some years, I became one of the owners. I was not rich, but I had enough money to live comfortably. I wrote 15 often to Biddy and Joe. I heard that Estella had married Drummle, and that he was very cruel to her.

At last, after eleven years, I came back to England. I went at once to my old home by the forge.

There, smoking his pipe in the old place by the 20 kitchen fire, sat Joe. He was as big and strong as ever. But his hair was now grey. Then I saw a little boy, sitting by the fire. He looked just like me, when I was a little boy. This was Joe's son.

'We named him Pip after you, dear old boy,' said Joe. 25 'We hope he grows up to be like you.'

A changed woman

In the evening, I went to look at Miss Havisham's house. As I came near it, I saw Estella coming towards me.

'I'm surprised that you still know me,' she said. 'I've 30 changed a lot.'

I looked at her face. Yes, she had changed, but to me she was even more beautiful. Her eyes were no longer cold and proud. They were filled with sadness and feeling.

She told me that her husband, Drummle, had died. She had sold the house. She had come to see it for the last time.

'And do you still live abroad?' she asked me.

'Yes, still,' I answered. 'I have to work hard, but I'm doing quite well.'

'I often thought of you,' she said.

'I always thought of you,' I replied. Then we were silent. After a while, Estella spoke.

'I'm saying goodbye to this place. But I'm not sad. I'm glad to leave it.'

'Are you, Estella?' I asked. 'For me, saying goodbye is very painful. When we said goodbye the last time, it was the end of all my dreams.'

'Dear Pip. At that time I didn't know what cruelty was. But I've learned the truth since then. My life has been very difficult to bear. I've been beaten and broken, but — I hope — I'm a better person for it. Please forgive me. Tell me we're friends.'

'Yes, we're friends.'

'And we'll still be friends … even when we say goodbye,' she said, smiling sadly.

But as we walked away from the house together, her hand was in mine. I knew that we would never say goodbye again.

QUESTIONS AND ACTIVITIES

CHAPTER 1

Put these sentences in the right order.

1 He went into the forge and got one of Joe's files.
2 Next morning Pip took a pie from the kitchen.
3 He thought he saw the prisoner, but it was someone else.
4 Pip met an escaped prisoner in the churchyard.
5 He found his prisoner waiting for him in the old building.
6 He poured some brandy into an empty bottle.
7 He promised to get him a file and some food.

CHAPTER 2

*Put these words in the right gaps: **river, brandy, find, friend, blacksmith, escaped, stared, soldiers, turned, village, trouble, searching, officer, caught, strange, stolen.***

Pip, Joe and Mr Wopsle went with the (1) _____ to watch them (2) _____ for the (3) _____ prisoners. Pip hoped they would not (4) _____ them. When both were (5) _____, Pip wanted his prisoner to know he was still his (6) _____. The prisoner (7) _____ at Pip in a (8) _____ way. Later, in the hut by the (9) _____, the prisoner (10) _____ to the (11) _____ and said he did not want anyone to get into (12) _____ because of him. He said he had (13) _____ some bread, (14) _____ and a pie from the (15) _____'s house in the (16) _____.

CHAPTER 3

Find the ten errors in this description of Miss Havisham.

Miss Havisham was the strangest lady Pip had ever seen. She was sitting in a large bed. Her head was resting on her knees. She was dressed all in white from her head to her fingers. Even her skin was white; and on top of it she wore a short veil. She wore only one glove: the other was on the table. She told Pip she had not gone out of the room for many months. She had not seen the sun since she was born. She touched the left side of her chest and told Pip that her heart was broken.

CHAPTER 4

Choose the right words to say what this part of the story is about.

Pip told Miss Havisham he was going to be a (1) **soldier/blacksmith** when he was (2) **older/younger.** Mrs Joe and Mr Pumblechook (3) **knew/hoped** she would (4) **give/lend** Pip some money to be (5) **an apprentice/a gentleman.** Joe did not want Pip to leave (6) **the forge/ Miss Havisham.** Pip was never (7) **sad/happy** at home. His (8) **mother/sister** was (9) **unkind/kind** to him, and Pip was (10) **ashamed/proud** of their rough, poor home.

CHAPTER 5

What should these words say?

Mr Jaggers said Pip would (1) **reinith** a lot of money. The person who was giving him this (2) **entrouf** wanted him to leave the (3) **goref**. That person wanted Pip to learn to be a (4) **ementlang**, and to have good (5) **nansrem** and a good (6) **undaicote**. Pip thought his (7) **emdar** had come true and that the (8) **wonnunk** person must be Miss Havisham. But Mr Jaggers said Pip must not try to find out who that (9) **nespor** was. Then Mr Jaggers gave Pip twenty (10) **donsup** for some new clothes. He said Pip could take a (11) **hocca** to London in (12) **tyxlace** one week's time and go to see him.

CHAPTER 6

Put the words at the ends of these sentences in the right order.

1 Miss Havisham's father   [rich] [a] [was] [man] [very].

2 When he died, he left his   [children] [to [money] [his] [both].

3 Miss Havisham's share was   [than] [more] [much] [brother's] [her].

4 The man she loved was   [interested] [her] [only] [in] [money].

5 Matthew Pocket told her   [man] [truth] [about] [the] [the].

6 She ordered Matthew to   [house] [at] [her] [leave] [once].

7 Since then   [hadn't] [each] [they] [other] [seen].

8 On the wedding day, the   [a] [man] [sent] [letter] [her].

9 It said that he no   [to] [her] [longer] [marry] [wanted].

10 He could not marry her   [already] [he] [married] [because] [was].

CHAPTER 7

Which of these sentences are true, and which are false?

1 A man came to Pip's rooms.
2 He was dressed in warm, thick clothes.
3 His hair was long and brown.
4 He looked as if he had been at sea for a long time.
5 He was about seventy years old, but he looked very strong.
6 The man held out both his hands to Pip, as to an old friend.
7 He said he had wanted to meet Pip for a long time.
8 He said he had forgotten Pip's kindness.
9 He had been a farmer in Australia, and grown rich.
10 He was now famous for his sheep.

CHAPTER 8

Put the underlined (b) sentences in the right paragraphs.

1   (a) It was not safe for Provis to leave Australia. (b) <u>There was a woman who came to clean the place.</u> (c) If the police found out that Provis had returned, he would be hanged.

2   (a) Pip could not hide Provis in his rooms. (b) <u>He did not know how he could pay back what he owed.</u> (c) The woman would talk about him to other people.

3   (a) Pip decided to find Provis a room in a house nearby. (b) <u>He had been sent there for the rest of his life.</u> (c) After he got the room, he went to see Mr Jaggers.

4   (a) Pip said he would not take any more money from Provis. (b) <u>It seemed the safest thing to do.</u> (c) Herbert said that Pip could go and work with him.

CHAPTER 9

Put the names in the right gaps. Choose from: **Miss Clara**, **Wemmick**, **Pip**, **Herbert**, **Provis**.

Wemmick said some people had found out that (1) _____ had left Australia. They had guessed he would come to (2) _____, and they had been watching (3) _____'s rooms. (4) _____ had said (5) _____ could stay in (6) _____'s house. (7) _____ thought this was a good plan. (8) _____'s house was near the river, so it would be easy to get (9) _____ to a ship when it was safe. (10) _____ told (11) _____ he would have to leave England soon. Then (12) _____ had another idea, which was to get a boat ready so that he and (13) _____ could row (14) _____ down the river themselves.

CHAPTER 10

Put the beginnings of these sentences with the right endings.

1 They rowed to where	(a) held on to the side of Pip's boat.
2 Then another boat	(b) had been badly hurt.
3 The men in the other boat	(c) was pulled into the other boat.

4 The *Hamburg*   (d) the steamships would pass by.

5 Both the small boats   (e) slipped and fell into the water.

6 Provis   (f) crossed in front of them.

7 Compeyson   (g) jumped into the other boat.

8 Pip's boat sank and he   (h) began to rock in the rough water.

9 Then Pip saw that Provis   (i) moved directly towards them.

CHAPTER 11

Who did or said these things? Choose from: **Pip, Estella, Provis, Miss Havisham, Drummle, Joe, Biddy.**

1 Who was happy because someone felt at ease with him?
2 Whose illness made him dream strange dreams?
3 Who felt hurt when someone called him 'sir'?
4 Who died from sitting too near to a candle?
5 Who cried because someone was so pale and thin?
6 Who married the best wife in the whole world?
7 Whose eyes were no longer cold and proud?
8 Who was very cruel to his wife?
9 Who would never say goodbye again?

GRADE 1

Alice's Adventures in Wonderland
Lewis Carroll

The Call of the Wild and Other Stories
Jack London

Emma
Jane Austen

The Golden Goose and Other Stories
Retold by David Foulds

Jane Eyre
Charlotte Brontë

Just So Stories
Rudyard Kipling

Little Women
Louisa M. Alcott

The Lost Umbrella of Kim Chu
Eleanor Estes

The Secret Garden
Frances Hodgson Burnett

Tales From the Arabian Nights
Edited by David Foulds

Treasure Island
Robert Louis Stevenson

The Wizard of Oz
L. Frank Baum

GRADE 2

The Adventures of Sherlock Holmes
Sir Arthur Conan Doyle

A Christmas Carol
Charles Dickens

The Dagger and Wings and Other Father Brown Stories
G.K. Chesterton

The Flying Heads and Other Strange Stories
Edited by David Foulds

The Golden Touch and Other Stories
Edited by David Foulds

Gulliver's Travels — A Voyage to Lilliput
Jonathan Swift

The Jungle Book
Rudyard Kipling

Life Without Katy and Other Stories
O. Henry

Lord Jim
Joseph Conrad

A Midsummer Night's Dream and Other Stories from Shakespeare's Plays
Edited by David Foulds

Oliver Twist
Charles Dickens

The Mill on the Floss
George Eliot

Nicholas Nickleby
Charles Dickens

The Prince and the Pauper
Mark Twain

The Stone Junk and Other Stories
D.H. Howe

Stories from Greek Tragedies
Retold by Kieran McGovern

Stories from Shakespeare's Comedies
Retold by Katherine Mattock

Tales of King Arthur
Retold by David Foulds

The Talking Tree and Other Stories
David McRobbie

Through the Looking Glass
Lewis Carroll

GRADE 3

The Adventures of Huckleberry Finn
Mark Twain

The Adventures of Tom Sawyer
Mark Twain

Around the World in Eighty Days
Jules Verne

The Canterville Ghost and Other Stories
Oscar Wilde

David Copperfield
Charles Dickens

Fog and Other Stories
Bill Lowe

Further Adventures of Sherlock Holmes
Sir Arthur Conan Doyle

Great Expectations
Charles Dickens

Gulliver's Travels — Further Voyages
Jonathan Swift